METRO BOOKS
New York

An Imprint of Sterling Publishing
387 Park Avenue South
New York, NY 10016

METRO BOOKS and the distinctive Metro Books logo are trademarks of Sterling Publishing Co., Inc.

© 2012 by ACP Magazines Ltd.

This 2012 edition published by Metro Books by arrangement with ACP Magazines Ltd.

All rights reserved. No part of this publication may be reproduced, stored in a retrieval system, or transmitted, in any form or by any means, electronic, mechanical, photocopying, recording, or otherwise, without prior written permission from the publisher.

ISBN 978-1-4351-4200-8

For information about custom editions, special sales, and premium and corporate purchases, please contact Sterling Special Sales at 800-805-5489 or specialsales@sterlingpublishing.com.

Manufactured in China

6 8 10 9 7 5

www.sterlingpublishing.com

The AFTERNOON TEA Collection

METRO BOOKS
New York

Contents

the teatime experience 6
sandwiches 8
scones 22
friands 32
little tarts 44
little cakes 68
big cakes 92
biscuits 138
slices 202
glossary 248
conversion chart 252
index 253

The teatime experience

Afternoon tea is a celebration of all things delightful and delectable, pretty and feminine. Set the table with a white tablecloth, fine china teacups, polished silverware and simply arranged flowers. The tiered serving stand is an essential accoutrement. Laden with little sandwiches, scones, pastries and tarts it is the centrepiece of the table, and the pièce de résistance of the teatime experience. And when the doorbell rings, it's time to put the kettle on.

Sandwiches

Afternoon tea always starts with sandwiches. Usually they're little finger sandwiches with the crusts cut off and a simple subtle filling, but they can also be cut into triangles. Make sure you don't overfill tea sandwiches – they should be delicate and one or two mouthfuls only.

sandwiches

chicken and almond sandwiches

1 cup (250ml) chicken stock
1 cup (250ml) water
6 black peppercorns
1 bay leaf
250g (8 ounces) chicken breast
1 stalk celery (150g), trimmed, chopped finely
2 tablespoons flaked almonds, roasted
¼ cup (60g) crème fraîche
2 tablespoons whole-egg mayonnaise
1 teaspoon lemon juice
2 teaspoons finely chopped fresh tarragon
30g (1 ounce) butter, softened
8 slices light rye bread (360g)

1 Combine stock, the water, peppercorns, bay leaf and chicken in small saucepan; bring to the boil. Reduce heat; simmer, uncovered, about 15 minutes or until chicken is cooked through, turning chicken halfway through cooking time. Remove chicken from poaching liquid. When cool enough to handle, chop chicken finely.
2 Combine chicken in medium bowl with celery, nuts, crème fraîche, mayonnaise, juice and tarragon. Season to taste.
3 Spread butter over bread slices; top half the slices with chicken mixture then remaining bread. Cut crusts from bread; cut each sandwich into three finger sandwiches, then cut each in half crossways into squares.

prep + cook time
35 minutes (+ cooling)
makes 24

marinated cucumber sandwiches

The cucumber can be sliced with a vegetable peeler for even, thin slices.

2 lebanese cucumbers (260g), sliced thinly lengthways
1 tablespoon white wine vinegar
1 tablespoon finely chopped fresh dill
½ teaspoon sea salt flakes
½ teaspoon caster (superfine) sugar
¼ teaspoon cracked black pepper
30g (1 ounce) butter, softened
8 slices wholemeal bread (360g)
½ cup (120g) crème fraîche

1 Combine cucumber, vinegar, dill, salt, sugar and pepper in medium bowl. Cover; refrigerate 2 hours.
2 Drain cucumber; discard excess liquid.
3 Spread butter over bread slices. Spread crème fraîche over half the buttered bread slices; top slices with cucumber then remaining bread. Cut crusts from bread; cut each sandwich into four fingers.

prep time 20 minutes (+ refrigeration)
makes 16

sandwiches

curried egg sandwiches

6 hard-boiled eggs,
  chopped coarsely
⅓ cup (100g) whole-egg
  mayonnaise
2 teaspoons curry powder
8 slices white bread (360g)
2 cups shredded iceberg lettuce

1 Use a fork to mash egg, mayonnaise and curry powder in medium bowl. Season to taste.
2 Spread egg mixture over half the bread slices; top with lettuce then remaining bread. Cut crusts from bread; cut each sandwich into four triangles.

prep time 15 minutes
makes 16

salmon and herbed cream cheese sandwiches

60g (2 ounces) cream cheese, softened
2 teaspoons each finely chopped fresh dill and chives
2 teaspoons lemon juice
1 teaspoon drained baby capers, rinsed, chopped finely
4 slices white bread (180g), crusts removed
125g (4 ounces) thinly sliced smoked salmon
4 large rocket (arugula) leaves, trimmed

1 Combine cream cheese, dill, chives, juice and capers in small bowl. Season to taste.
2 Using rolling pin, roll over one slice of bread to flatten slightly. Spread with a quarter of the cream cheese mixture; top with a quarter of the smoked salmon and one rocket leaf, roll tightly to enclose filling. Repeat with remaining bread, cream cheese mixture, smoked salmon and rocket. Trim ends then cut each roll into four pieces.

prep time 20 minutes
makes 16

sandwiches

prawn and lime pepper aïoli sandwiches

16 cooked medium king prawns (shrimp) (720g)
30g (1 ounce) butter, softened
8 slices white bread (360g)
1 cup (60g) shredded baby cos (romaine) lettuce

lime pepper aïoli
½ cup (150g) whole-egg mayonnaise
1 small clove garlic, crushed
½ teaspoon finely grated lime rind
2 teaspoons lime juice
¼ teaspoon cracked black pepper

1 Make lime pepper aïoli.
2 Shell and devein prawns; halve lengthways. Stir prawns into aïoli. Season to taste.
3 Spread butter over bread slices; top half the slices with prawn mixture and shredded lettuce then remaining bread. Cut crusts from bread; cut each sandwich into four triangles.
lime pepper aïoli Combine ingredients in medium bowl.

prep time 25 minutes
makes 16

chicken and celery sandwiches

3 cups (480g) finely chopped cooked chicken
4 green onions (scallions), chopped finely
½ cup (60g) finely chopped roasted walnuts
3 stalks celery (450g), trimmed, chopped finely
½ cup (150g) whole-egg mayonnaise
⅓ cup (80g) sour cream
20 slices white bread (900g)
10 slices wholemeal bread (450g)

1 Combine chicken, onion, nuts, celery, mayonnaise and sour cream in large bowl.
2 Spread half the chicken mixture onto half the white bread slices; top with wholemeal bread slices. Spread remaining chicken mixture onto wholemeal bread then top with remaining white bread slices. Cut crusts from bread; cut each sandwich into three fingers.

prep time 40 minutes
makes 30

Scones

At afternoon teas in country houses the tradition is to put the scones in the oven just as the guests arrive. Warm from the oven and served with jam and cream, fresh scones are an experience not to be missed. This lovely country tradition can be duplicated in your own home – make them no more than an hour before you cook them.

scones with jam and cream

Scones are best made on the day of serving. They can be frozen for up to 3 months. Thaw in oven, wrapped in foil. You could substitute the double cream for clotted cream or whipped thickened cream.

2½ cups (375g) self-raising flour
1 tablespoon caster (superfine) sugar
30g (1 ounce) butter, chopped
1¼ cups (310ml) buttermilk
¾ cup (240g) black cherry jam
1 cup (250ml) double (thick) cream

1 Preheat oven to 220°C/425°F. Grease 22cm (9-inch) square cake pan.
2 Sift flour and sugar into large bowl; rub in butter.
3 Add buttermilk. Use a knife to cut the buttermilk through the flour mixture to make a soft, sticky dough. Turn dough onto floured surface, knead gently until smooth.
4 Press dough out to 2cm (¾-inch) thickness, cut out 4cm (1½-inch) rounds. Place scones, just touching, in pan. Gently knead scraps of dough together; repeat process. Brush scones with a little extra buttermilk.
5 Bake scones about 15 minutes. Serve warm scones with jam and cream.

prep + cook time 35 minutes
makes 25

vanilla bean scones

Scones are best made on the day of serving. They can be frozen for up to 3 months. Thaw in oven, wrapped in foil. It is fine to use just one 300ml carton of cream for this recipe.

2½ cups (375g) self-raising flour
1 tablespoon caster (superfine) sugar
30g (1 ounce) butter, chopped
¾ cup (180ml) milk
½ cup (125ml) water
1 vanilla bean
1¼ cups (310ml) thickened (heavy) cream
2 tablespoons icing (confectioners') sugar
¾ cup (240g) strawberry jam
250g (8 ounces) strawberries, sliced thinly

1 Preheat oven to 220°C/425°F. Grease 22cm (9-inch) square cake pan.
2 Sift flour and caster sugar into large bowl; rub in butter.
3 Combine milk and the water in a medium jug. Split vanilla bean open and scrape seeds into milk mixture; discard bean. Add milk mixture to flour mixture; use a knife to cut the milk mixture through the flour mixture to make a soft, sticky dough. Turn dough onto floured surface, knead gently until smooth.
4 Press dough out to 20cm (8-inch) square, cut into 16 squares using floured knife. Place squares, just touching, in pan. Brush scones with a little extra milk.
5 Bake scones about 20 minutes.
6 Meanwhile, beat cream and half the sifted icing sugar in small bowl with electric mixer until soft peaks form.
7 Sandwich warm scones with jam, strawberries and cream; serve dusted with remaining sifted icing sugar.

prep + cook time 40 minutes
makes 16

date scones with whipped caramel butter

Scones are best made on the day of serving. They can be frozen for up to 3 months. Thaw in oven, wrapped in foil.

30g (1 ounce) butter, softened
¼ cup (55g) firmly packed brown sugar
1 egg yolk
2½ cups (375g) self-raising flour
⅓ cup (50g) finely chopped seeded dried dates
1¼ cups (310ml) buttermilk

whipped caramel butter
150g (5 ounces) unsalted butter, softened
¼ cup (55g) brown sugar
2 teaspoons vanilla extract

1 Preheat oven to 220°C/425°F. Grease 22cm (9-inch) square cake pan.
2 Beat butter, sugar and egg yolk in small bowl with electric mixer until light and fluffy. Transfer mixture to large bowl; add sifted flour, dates and buttermilk. Use a knife to cut the buttermilk through the flour mixture to make a soft, sticky dough. Turn dough onto floured surface, knead gently until smooth.
3 Press dough out to 20cm (8-inch) square, cut into nine squares, using a floured knife, then cut each square in half diagonally. Place scones side by side, just touching, in pan. Brush scones with a little extra buttermilk.
4 Bake scones about 20 minutes.
5 Meanwhile, make whipped caramel butter.
6 Serve warm scones with whipped caramel butter.
whipped caramel butter Beat ingredients in small bowl with electric mixer until light and fluffy.

prep + cook time 40 minutes
makes 18

gingerbread scones with lemon glacé icing

Scones are best made on the day of serving. They can be frozen for up to 3 months. Thaw in oven, wrapped in foil. Use a zester to shred lemon rind.

30g (1 ounce) butter, softened
¼ cup (55g) firmly packed light brown sugar
1 egg yolk
2½ cups (375g) self-raising flour
3 teaspoons ground ginger
1½ teaspoons ground cinnamon
¼ teaspoon ground cloves
1 cup (250ml) buttermilk
2 tablespoons treacle or golden syrup

lemon glacé icing
1 cup (160g) icing (confectioners') sugar
15g (½ ounce) butter, melted
1 tablespoon lemon juice, approximately

1 Preheat oven to 220°C/425°F. Grease 22cm (9-inch) square cake pan.
2 Beat butter, sugar and egg yolk in small bowl with electric mixer until light and fluffy. Transfer mixture to large bowl; add sifted dry ingredients and combined buttermilk and treacle. Use a knife to cut the buttermilk mixture through flour mixture to make a soft, sticky dough. Turn dough onto floured surface, knead gently until smooth.
3 Press dough out to 2cm (¾-inch) thickness, cut into 5cm (2-inch) rounds. Place rounds, just touching, in pan. Gently knead scraps of dough together; repeat process. Brush scones with a little extra buttermilk.
4 Bake scones about 20 minutes. Cool 10 minutes.
5 Meanwhile, make lemon glacé icing.
6 Serve warm scones drizzled with icing and decorated with shredded lemon rind, if you like.

lemon glacé icing Sift icing sugar into small heatproof bowl; stir in butter and enough juice to make a thick paste. Place bowl over small saucepan of simmering water; stir until mixture is smooth.

prep + cook time 40 minutes
makes 16

Friands

Essentially little cakes made with egg whites and ground nuts, friands look very impressive on the tea table. There are special friand pans you can buy at kitchenware shops but they work just as well if you make them in muffin pans or patty pans.

friands

orange blossom friands

We used tart moulds bought from a supermarket, which came in sets of four. The friand mixture will be fine left to stand at room temperature if you're making the friands in small batches. Alternatively, make 12 friands using 12-hole (½-cup/125ml) oval friand pan. Divide mixture into pan holes, bake about 20 minutes.

6 egg whites
185g (6 ounces) unsalted butter, melted
2 tablespoons honey
1 tablespoon orange blossom water
1 cup (120g) ground almonds
1½ cups (240g) icing (confectioners') sugar
½ cup (75g) plain (all-purpose) flour
½ cup (40g) flaked almonds
honey syrup
2 tablespoons honey
1 tablespoon water
2 teaspoons orange blossom water

1 Preheat oven to 200°C/400°F. Grease individual fluted tart moulds (1½-tablespoon/30ml) with butter. Place on oven tray.
2 Place egg whites in medium bowl; whisk lightly with fork until combined. Add butter, honey, orange blossom water, ground almonds, sifted icing sugar and flour; stir until combined. Half fill the tart moulds with mixture; sprinkle with almonds.
3 Bake friands about 12 minutes. Stand friands 5 minutes before turning top-side up onto wire rack to cool. Repeat with remaining mixture and almonds.
4 Meanwhile, make honey syrup.
5 Serve friands drizzled with honey syrup.
honey syrup Combine honey and the water in small saucepan; bring to the boil. Remove from heat; stir in orange blossom water. Cool.

prep + cook time
35 minutes (+ cooling)
makes 28

fig and walnut friands

1¼ cups (125g) roasted walnuts
6 egg whites
185g (6 ounces) unsalted butter, melted
1½ cups (240g) icing (confectioners') sugar
½ cup (75g) plain (all-purpose) flour
2 teaspoons finely grated orange rind
1 tablespoon orange juice
4 dried figs (85g), sliced thinly

1 Preheat oven to 200°C/400°F. Grease 12-hole (½-cup/125ml) oval friand pan.
2 Process nuts until ground finely.
3 Place egg whites in medium bowl; whisk lightly with fork until combined. Add butter, sifted icing sugar and flour, rind, juice and nuts; stir until combined. Divide mixture into pans, top with slices of fig.
4 Bake friands about 20 minutes. Stand friands 5 minutes before turning top-side up onto wire rack to cool. Serve dusted with a little sifted icing sugar.

prep + cook time 35 minutes
makes 12

friands

mandarin and poppy seed friands

Store friands in an airtight container for up to three days.

2 large mandarins (500g)
1 tablespoon poppy seeds
6 egg whites
185g (6 ounces) butter, melted
1 cup (120g) ground almonds
1½ cups (240g) icing (confectioners') sugar
½ cup (75g) plain (all-purpose) flour

1 Preheat oven to 200°C/400°F. Line 12-hole (½-cup/125ml) oval friand pan with paper cases.
2 Finely grate rind from mandarins (you will need 2 tablespoons of rind). Juice the mandarins (you will need 2 tablespoons of juice).
3 Combine poppy seeds and juice in small jug; stand 10 minutes.
4 Place egg whites in medium bowl; whisk lightly with fork until combined. Add butter, ground almonds, sifted icing sugar and flour, rind and poppy seed mixture; stir until combined. Divide mixture into paper cases.
5 Bake friands about 20 minutes. Stand friands 5 minutes before turning, top-side up, onto wire rack to cool. Serve lightly dusted with sifted icing sugar.

prep + cook time 35 minutes
makes 12

lemon and cranberry friands

Store friands in an airtight container for up to three days.

6 egg whites
185g (6 ounces) butter, melted
1 cup (120g) ground almonds
1½ cups (240g) icing (confectioners') sugar
½ cup (75g) plain (all-purpose) flour
¾ cup (105g) dried cranberries
1 tablespoon finely grated lemon rind
1 tablespoon lemon juice

1 Preheat oven to 200°C/400°F. Grease 12-hole (½-cup/125ml) oval friand pan.
2 Place egg whites in medium bowl; whisk lightly with fork until combined. Add butter, ground almonds, sifted icing sugar and flour, berries, rind and juice; stir until combined. Divide mixture into pan holes.
3 Bake friands about 20 minutes. Stand friands 5 minutes before turning, top-side up, onto wire rack to cool. Serve lightly dusted with sifted icing sugar.

prep + cook time 35 minutes
makes 12

pistachio and lime friands

Store friands in an airtight container for up to three days. We used freeform paper cases made by pushing a 12cm (4¾-inch) square of paper (we used paper about the same thickness as printer paper) into ungreased pan holes, followed by a 12cm (4¾-inch) square of baking paper.

1 cup (140g) roasted unsalted pistachios
6 egg whites
185g (6 ounces) butter, melted
1½ cups (240g) icing (confectioners') sugar
½ cup (75g) plain (all-purpose) flour
2 teaspoons finely grated lime rind
1 tablespoon lime juice

1 Preheat oven to 200°C/400°F. Line 12-hole (½-cup/125ml) oval friand pan.
2 Process nuts until ground finely.
3 Place egg whites in medium bowl; whisk lightly with fork until combined. Add butter, sifted icing sugar and flour, rind, juice and nuts; stir until combined. Divide mixture into pan holes.
4 Bake friands about 25 minutes. Stand friands 5 minutes before turning, top-side up, onto wire rack to cool. Serve dusted with a little sifted icing sugar.

prep + cook time 40 minutes
makes 12

Little Tarts

Little tarts are the prettiest things on the tea table. Custard tarts, fruit tarts, chocolate tarts, lemon tarts – they're all absolutely irresistible. It's wise to make more than you think you'll need – you can be sure there will be none left at the end of teatime.

little tarts

custard fruit flans

Pastry cases and custard cream can be made and stored separately, two days ahead; fold cream into custard just before using. Assemble and serve flans as close to serving as possible – about an hour is good.

1¾ cups (260g) plain (all-purpose) flour
¼ cup (40g) icing (confectioners') sugar
185g (6 ounces) cold butter, chopped coarsely
1 egg yolk
2 teaspoons iced water, approximately
1 medium kiwifruit (85g)
60g (2 ounces) fresh raspberries, halved
60g (2 ounces) fresh blueberries

custard cream
1 cup (250ml) milk
1 teaspoon vanilla extract
3 egg yolks
⅓ cup (75g) caster (superfine) sugar
2 tablespoons pure cornflour (cornstarch)
⅓ cup (80ml) thickened (heavy) cream, whipped

1 Process flour, sugar and butter until crumbly. With motor operating, add egg yolk and enough of the water to make ingredients come together. Turn dough onto floured surface, knead gently until smooth. Wrap pastry in plastic; refrigerate 30 minutes.
2 Grease two 12-hole (1-tablespoon/20ml) mini muffin pans. Roll out half the pastry between sheets of baking paper until 3mm (⅛ inch) thick. Cut out 12 x 6cm (2¼-inch) rounds; press rounds into holes of one pan. Prick bases of cases well with a fork. Repeat with remaining pastry. Refrigerate 30 minutes.
3 Preheat oven to 220°C/425°F.
4 Bake cases about 12 minutes. Stand cases 5 minutes before transferring to wire rack to cool.
5 Meanwhile, make custard cream.
6 Cut kiwifruit crossways into eight slices; cut 3cm (1¼-inch) rounds from slices. Divide custard cream into cases; top with fruit.

custard cream Combine milk and extract in small saucepan; bring to the boil. Meanwhile, beat egg yolks, sugar and cornflour in small bowl with electric mixer until thick. With motor operating, gradually beat in hot milk mixture. Return custard to pan; stir over heat until mixture boils and thickens. Cover surface of custard with plastic wrap, refrigerate 1 hour. Fold cream into custard, in two batches.

prep + cook time
1 hour (+ refrigeration & cooling)
makes 24

limoncello meringue pies

Pastry cases and curd can be made 2 days ahead. Store the cases in an airtight container and the curd in the refrigerator.

1¾ cups (260g) plain (all-purpose) flour
¼ cup (40g) icing (confectioners') sugar
185g (6 ounces) cold unsalted butter, chopped coarsely
1 egg yolk
2 teaspoons iced water, approximately
3 egg whites
¾ cup (165g) caster (superfine) sugar

limoncello curd
3 egg yolks
½ cup (110g) caster (superfine) sugar
1 teaspoon finely grated lemon rind
¼ cup (60ml) lemon juice
90g (3 ounces) cold unsalted butter, chopped
1 tablespoon limoncello liqueur

1 Make limoncello curd.
2 Process flour, icing sugar and butter until crumbly. With motor operating, add egg yolk and enough of the water to make ingredients come together. Turn dough onto floured surface, knead gently until smooth. Wrap pastry in plastic; refrigerate 30 minutes.
3 Grease two 12-hole (1-tablespoon/20ml) mini muffin pans. Roll out half the pastry between sheets of baking paper until 5mm (¼ inch) thick. Cut out 12 x 6cm (2¼-inch) rounds; press rounds into holes of one pan. Prick base of cases well with a fork. Repeat with remaining pastry. Refrigerate 30 minutes.
4 Meanwhile, preheat oven to 220°C/425°F.
5 Bake cases about 12 minutes. Stand cases 5 minutes before transferring to wire rack to cool.
6 Beat egg whites in small bowl with electric mixer until soft peaks form. Gradually add caster sugar, beating until dissolved between additions.
7 Increase oven to 240°C/475°F.
8 Divide limoncello curd into cases. Spoon meringue mixture into piping bag fitted with 1cm (½-inch) plain tube; pipe meringue over curd.
9 Bake pies about 2 minutes. Cool.

limoncello curd Whisk egg yolks and sugar in medium heatproof bowl until pale and thickened slightly. Whisk in rind and juice; stir over medium saucepan of simmering water about 12 minutes or until mixture coats the back of a spoon. Remove from heat; gradually whisk in butter until combined between additions. Stir in limoncello; cover, refrigerate overnight.

prep + cook time
1 hour 15 minutes
(+ refrigeration & cooling)
makes 24

little tarts

cherry bakewell tarts

90g (3 ounces) unsalted butter, softened
2 tablespoons caster (superfine) sugar
1 egg yolk
1 cup (150g) plain (all-purpose) flour
½ cup (60g) ground almonds
2 tablespoons strawberry jam
12 red glacé cherries, halved

almond filling
125g (4 ounces) unsalted butter, softened
½ teaspoon finely grated lemon rind
½ cup (110g) caster (superfine) sugar
2 eggs
¾ cup (90g) ground almonds
2 tablespoons plain (all-purpose) flour

lemon glaze
1 cup (160g) icing (confectioners') sugar
2 tablespoons lemon juice, approximately

1 Beat butter, sugar and egg yolk in small bowl with electric mixer until combined. Stir in sifted flour and ground almonds in two batches. Turn dough onto floured surface, knead gently until smooth, wrap in plastic; refrigerate 30 minutes.
2 Preheat oven to 220°C/425°F.
3 Make almond filling.
4 Grease two 12-hole (1½-tablespoons/30ml) shallow round-based patty pans. Roll pastry between sheets of baking paper until 3mm (⅛ inch) thick. Cut 24 x 6cm (2¼-inch) rounds from pastry; gently press rounds into holes in pans. Spoon jam then filling into cases.
5 Bake tarts about 20 minutes. Stand tarts 10 minutes; turn, top-side up, onto wire rack.
6 Meanwhile, make lemon glaze.
7 Spoon glaze over warm tarts; top with cherries. Cool.

almond filling Beat butter, rind and sugar in small bowl with electric mixer until light and fluffy. Beat in eggs, one at a time. Stir in ground almonds and flour.
lemon glaze Sift icing sugar into small bowl, stir in enough juice to make glaze pourable.

prep + cook time
1 hour (+ refrigeration & cooling)
makes 24

neenish and pineapple tarts

1¾ cups (260g) plain (all-purpose) flour
¼ cup (40g) icing (confectioners') sugar
185g (6 ounces) cold butter, chopped coarsely
1 egg yolk
2 teaspoons iced water, approximately
2 tablespoons strawberry jam
2 tablespoons finely chopped glacé pineapple

mock cream
¾ cup (165g) caster (superfine) sugar
1½ tablespoons milk
⅓ cup (80ml) water
½ teaspoon gelatine
185g (6 ounces) unsalted butter, softened
1 teaspoon vanilla extract

glacé icing
1½ cups (240g) icing (confectioners') sugar
15g (½ ounce) unsalted butter, melted
2 tablespoons hot milk, approximately
yellow and pink food colouring
½ teaspoon cocoa powder

1 Process flour, sugar and butter until crumbly. With motor operating, add egg yolk and enough of the water to make ingredients come together. Turn dough onto floured surface, knead gently until smooth. Wrap pastry in plastic; refrigerate 30 minutes.

2 Grease two 12-hole (2-tablespoons/40ml) deep flat-based patty pans. Roll out half the pastry between sheets of baking paper until 3mm (⅛ inch) thick. Cut out 12 x 7.5cm (3-inch) rounds; press rounds into holes of one pan. Prick bases of cases well with a fork. Repeat with remaining pastry. Refrigerate 30 minutes.

3 Preheat oven to 220°C/425°F.

4 Bake cases about 12 minutes. Stand cases 5 minutes before transferring to wire rack to cool.

5 Meanwhile, make mock cream and glacé icing.

6 Divide jam among half the cases and pineapple among remaining cases. Fill cases with mock cream, level tops with spatula. Spread yellow icing over pineapple tarts. Spread pink icing over half of each jam tart; spread remaining half with chocolate icing.

mock cream Stir sugar, milk and ¼ cup of the water in small saucepan over low heat, without boiling, until sugar dissolves. Sprinkle gelatine over remaining water in small jug; stir into milk mixture until gelatine dissolves. Cool to room temperature. Beat butter and extract in small bowl with electric mixer until as white as possible. With motor operating, gradually beat in cold milk mixture; beat until light and fluffy.

glacé icing Sift icing sugar into medium bowl; stir in butter and enough of the milk to make a thick paste. Place ⅔ cup of the icing in small heatproof bowl; tint with yellow colouring. Divide remaining icing between two small heatproof bowls; tint icing in one bowl with pink colouring and the other with sifted cocoa. Stir each bowl over small saucepan of simmering water until icing is spreadable.

prep + cook time
1 hour 10 minutes
(+ refrigeration & cooling)
makes 24

little tarts

rhubarb frangipane tarts

1 vanilla bean
½ cup (110g) caster (superfine) sugar
¼ cup (60ml) water
10 stalks trimmed rhubarb (300g), cut into 4cm (1½-inch) lengths
40g (1½ ounces) butter, softened
2 tablespoons caster (superfine) sugar, extra
½ teaspoon vanilla extract
1 egg yolk
½ cup (60g) ground almonds
2 teaspoons plain (all-purpose) flour
1 sheet butter puff pastry

1 Preheat oven to 180°C/350°F. Grease two oven trays.
2 Split vanilla bean, scrape seeds into a small saucepan; discard bean. Add sugar and the water to the pan. Stir syrup over heat, without boiling, until sugar dissolves. Combine rhubarb and syrup in medium baking dish; bake, uncovered, 15 minutes or until rhubarb is tender. Cool. Drain rhubarb; reserve syrup.
3 Meanwhile, beat butter, extra sugar, extract and egg yolk in small bowl with electric mixer until light and fluffy. Stir in ground almonds and flour.

4 Cut pastry into quarters; cut each quarter into three rectangles. Place pastry rectangles about 5cm (2 inches) apart on trays; spread rounded teaspoons of almond mixture over each rectangle, leaving a 5mm (¼-inch) border. Top with rhubarb; fold pastry edges in towards centre to form raised border.
5 Bake tarts about 25 minutes. Serve tarts warm, brushed with reserved syrup.

prep + cook time
1 hour 10 minutes (+ cooling)
makes 12

passionfruit curd and coconut tarts

1¾ cups (260g) plain (all-purpose) flour
¼ cup (40g) icing (confectioners') sugar
¼ cup (20g) desiccated coconut
185g (6 ounces) cold unsalted butter, chopped coarsely
1 egg yolk
2 teaspoons iced water, approximately
1 small coconut (700g)

passionfruit curd
⅓ cup (80ml) passionfruit pulp
½ cup (110g) caster (superfine) sugar
2 eggs, beaten lightly
125g (4 ounces) unsalted butter, chopped coarsely

1 Make passionfruit curd.
2 Process flour, sugar, desiccated coconut and butter until crumbly. With motor operating, add egg yolk and enough of the water to make ingredients come together. Turn dough onto floured surface, knead gently until smooth. Wrap pastry in plastic; refrigerate 30 minutes.
3 Grease two 12-hole (2-tablespoon/40ml) deep flat-based patty pans. Roll out half the pastry between sheets of baking paper until 5mm (¼ inch) thick. Cut out 12 x 7.5cm (3-inch) rounds; press rounds into holes of one pan. Prick bases of cases well with a fork. Repeat with remaining pastry. Refrigerate 30 minutes.
4 Preheat oven to 220°C/425°F.
5 Bake cases about 12 minutes or until browned. Stand cases 5 minutes before transferring to wire rack to cool.
6 Increase oven to 240°C/475°F. Pierce one eye of the coconut using sharp knife; drain liquid from coconut. Place coconut on oven tray; bake about 10 minutes or until cracks appear. Carefully split the coconut open by hitting with a hammer; remove flesh. Using vegetable peeler, slice coconut into curls; reserve ½ cup coconut curls for this recipe and keep remaining for another use. Roast reserved coconut on oven tray about 5 minutes or until lightly browned.
7 Divide passionfruit curd into cases; top with coconut curls.

passionfruit curd Stir ingredients in medium heatproof bowl over medium saucepan of simmering water about 10 minutes or until mixture coats the back of a wooden spoon. Cover surface with plastic wrap; refrigerate overnight.

prep + cook time
1 hour 10 minutes
(+ refrigeration & cooling)
makes 24

portuguese custard tarts

Make tarts ahead (day before). Store in an airtight container. Re-crisp in 220°C/425°F oven for 5 minutes.

½ cup (110g) caster (superfine) sugar
2 tablespoons cornflour (cornstarch)
3 egg yolks
¾ cup (180ml) milk
½ cup (125ml) pouring cream
1 vanilla bean
5cm (2-inch) strip lemon rind
1 sheet butter puff pastry

1 Preheat oven to 220°C/425°F. Grease two 12-hole (1-tablespoon /20ml) mini muffin pans.
2 Combine sugar and cornflour in medium saucepan. Gradually whisk in combined egg yolks, milk and cream to make custard.
3 Split vanilla bean, scrape seeds into custard; discard bean. Add rind; stir over heat until mixture comes to the boil. Strain custard into medium jug. Cover surface of custard with plastic while making pastry cases.
4 Cut pastry sheet in half; place the two halves on top of each other. Roll pastry up tightly from long side; cut log into 24 rounds. Roll each pastry round on floured surface until 6cm (2¼ inches) in diameter. Press pastry rounds into pan holes.
5 Divide custard between cases.
6 Bake tarts about 12 minutes. Turn tarts top-side up onto wire rack to cool. Dust with a little sifted icing sugar before serving, if you like.

prep + cook time 45 minutes
makes 24

lemon crème brûlée tarts

Blowtorches are available from kitchenware and hardware stores. It is fine to use just one 300ml carton of cream for this recipe.

1¼ cups (310ml) pouring cream
⅓ cup (80ml) milk
4 x 5cm (2-inch) strips lemon rind
4 egg yolks
¼ cup (55g) caster (superfine) sugar

pastry
1¾ cups (260g) plain (all-purpose) flour
¼ cup (40g) icing (confectioners') sugar
2 teaspoons finely grated lemon rind
185g (6 ounces) cold butter, chopped coarsely
1 egg yolk
2 teaspoons iced water, approximately

toffee
1 cup (220g) caster (superfine) sugar
½ cup (125ml) water

1 Make pastry.
2 Grease two 12-hole (1½-tablespoon/30ml) shallow round-based patty pans. Roll half the pastry between sheets of baking paper to 3mm (⅛-inch) thickness. Cut out 12 x 6cm (2¼-inch) fluted rounds; press rounds into pan holes. Prick bases of cases well with a fork. Repeat with remaining pastry. Refrigerate 30 minutes.
3 Preheat oven to 160°C/325°F.
4 Bring cream, milk and rind to the boil in small saucepan. Beat egg yolks and sugar in small bowl with electric mixer until thick and creamy. Gradually beat hot cream mixture into egg mixture; allow bubbles to subside. Strain custard into medium jug, divide between cases.
5 Bake tarts about 25 minutes. Cool. Refrigerate tarts 2 hours.
6 Make toffee.
7 Remove tarts from pan; place on oven tray. Sprinkle custard with toffee; using blowtorch, heat until toffee caramelises.

pastry Process flour, sugar, rind and butter until crumbly. With motor operating, add egg yolk and enough of the water to make ingredients come together. Turn dough onto floured surface, knead gently until smooth. Wrap pastry in plastic; refrigerate 30 minutes.
toffee Stir sugar and the water in medium saucepan over heat, without boiling, until sugar dissolves. Bring to the boil. Boil, uncovered, without stirring, until golden brown. Pour toffee on greased oven tray to set. Break toffee into large pieces; process until chopped finely.

prep + cook time
1 hour 10 minutes
(+ refrigeration & cooling)
makes 24

little tarts

chocolate tartlets

If pastry is too dry, add 2 teaspoons of water with the egg yolk.

155g (5 ounces) dark eating (semi-sweet) chocolate, chopped coarsely
¼ cup (60ml) thickened (heavy) cream
1 tablespoon orange-flavoured liqueur
1 egg
2 egg yolks
2 tablespoons caster (superfine) sugar

pastry
1⅔ cups (250g) plain (all-purpose) flour
⅓ cup (75g) caster (superfine) sugar
10g (½ ounce) cold butter, chopped coarsely
1 egg yolk

1 Make pastry.
2 Grease two 12-hole (2-tablespoon/40ml) deep flat-based patty pans.
3 Roll pastry between sheets of baking paper to 3mm (⅛-inch) thickness; cut out 24 x 6.5cm (2¾-inch) rounds. Press rounds into pan holes; prick bases all over with fork. Refrigerate 30 minutes.
4 Preheat oven to 200°C/400°F.
5 Bake pastry cases 10 minutes. Cool. Reduce oven to 180°C/350°F.
6 Stir chocolate, cream and liqueur in small saucepan over low heat until smooth. Cool 5 minutes.
7 Meanwhile, beat egg, egg yolks and sugar in small bowl with electric mixer until light and fluffy; fold chocolate mixture into egg mixture.
8 Divide filling into pastry cases. Bake 8 minutes; cool 10 minutes. Refrigerate 1 hour.
9 Serve tartlets dusted with a little sifted cocoa powder.

pastry Process flour, sugar and butter until coarse. Add egg yolk; process until combined. Knead pastry on floured surface until smooth. Cover; refrigerate 30 minutes.

prep + cook time
50 minutes (+ refrigeration)
makes 24

crème brûlée praline tarts

If pastry is a little too dry, add 2 teaspoons of water with the egg yolk.

1¼ cups (185g) plain (all-purpose) flour
¼ cup (55g) caster (superfine) sugar
125g (4 ounces) cold butter, chopped coarsely
1 egg yolk
1⅓ cups (330ml) pouring cream
⅓ cup (80ml) milk
1 vanilla bean
4 egg yolks
¼ cup (55g) caster (superfine) sugar, extra

praline
¼ cup (55g) caster (superfine) sugar
2 tablespoons water
2 tablespoons roasted unsalted pistachios
1 tablespoon roasted hazelnuts

1 Process flour, sugar and butter until coarse. Add egg yolk; process until combined. Knead on floured surface until smooth. Roll pastry between sheets of baking paper until 4mm (⅛-inch) thick. Refrigerate 15 minutes.
2 Grease six-hole (¾-cup/180ml) texas muffin pan. Cut six 11cm (4½-inch) rounds from pastry. Press rounds into pan holes; prick bases with fork. Refrigerate 30 minutes.
3 Preheat oven to 160°C/350°F.
4 Combine cream and milk in small saucepan. Split vanilla bean in half lengthways; scrape seeds into pan (reserve pod for another use). Bring to the boil. Beat egg yolks and extra sugar in small bowl with electric mixer until thick and creamy. Gradually whisk hot cream mixture into egg mixture. Pour warm custard into pastry cases.
5 Bake tarts about 30 minutes or until set; cool 15 minutes. Refrigerate 1 hour.
6 Meanwhile, make praline.
7 Preheat grill (broiler).
8 Remove tarts from pan; place on oven tray. Sprinkle custard with praline; grill until praline caramelises. Serve immediately.

praline Stir sugar and the water in small saucepan over heat until sugar dissolves. Boil, uncovered, without stirring, about 8 minutes or until golden. Place nuts, in single layer, on greased oven tray. Pour toffee over nuts; stand 15 minutes or until set. Break toffee into pieces; process until fine.

prep + cook time
1 hour 15 minutes (+ refrigeration, standing & cooling)
makes 6

little tarts

caramel tarts

18 butternut snap biscuits (220g)
395g (12½ ounces) canned sweetened condensed milk
60g (2 ounces) butter, chopped coarsely
⅓ cup (75g) firmly packed light brown sugar
1 tablespoon lemon juice

1 Preheat oven to 160°C/325°F. Grease two 12-hole (1½-tablespoon/30ml) shallow round-based patty pans.
2 Place one biscuit each over top of 18 pan holes. Bake about 4 minutes or until biscuits soften. Using the back of a teaspoon, gently press softened biscuits into pan holes; cool.
3 Combine condensed milk, butter and sugar in small heavy-based saucepan; stir over heat until smooth. Bring to the boil; boil, stirring, about 10 minutes or until mixture is thick and dark caramel in colour. Remove from heat; stir in juice.
4 Divide mixture among biscuit cases; refrigerate 30 minutes or until set.

prep + cook time
35 minutes (+ refrigeration)
makes 18

Little Cakes

There's something incredibly satisfying about making and decorating little cakes. They're so pretty and luscious-looking and you can be as generous with the icing or filling as you like. Most little cakes are best made on the day they are to be eaten.

little cakes

mini sponge rolls

4 eggs
1¼ cups (150g) ground almonds
1 cup (160g) icing (confectioners') sugar
⅓ cup (50g) plain (all-purpose) flour
30g (1 ounce) unsalted butter, melted
4 egg whites
1 tablespoon caster (superfine) sugar
2 tablespoons desiccated coconut
1 tablespoon white (granulated) sugar
⅔ cup (220g) redcurrant jelly, warmed, strained

mock cream
½ cup (110g) caster (superfine) sugar
¼ cup (60ml) water
1 tablespoon milk
¼ teaspoon gelatine
125g (4 ounces) unsalted butter, softened
1 teaspoon vanilla extract

1 Preheat oven to 220°C/425°F. Mark three 20cm x 25cm (8-inch x 10-inch) rectangles on three sheets baking paper. Grease three oven trays; line with baking paper, marked-side down.

2 Beat eggs, ground almonds and sifted icing sugar in small bowl with electric mixer until creamy; beat in flour. Transfer mixture to large bowl; stir in butter.

3 Beat egg whites in clean small bowl with electric mixer until soft peaks form; add caster sugar, beat until dissolved. Fold into almond mixture, in two batches.

4 Divide mixture between trays, spread inside rectangles. Bake, one at a time, about 7 minutes.

5 Meanwhile, cut three pieces of baking paper the same size as the base of 26cm x 32cm (10-inch x 13-inch) swiss roll pan; place paper on bench. Sprinkle one piece of paper with half the coconut, one with half the white sugar and the other with combined remaining coconut and white sugar. Turn each sponge onto baking paper; peel away lining paper.

Cut crisp edges from all sides of sponges. Roll sponges from long side, using paper as guide; unroll, then cool.

6 Meanwhile, make mock cream.

7 Spread each sponge with cold jelly and mock cream, then re-roll sponges. Cover; refrigerate 30 minutes. Cut each roll into eight pieces.

mock cream Stir sugar, 2 tablespoons of the water and milk in small saucepan over low heat, without boiling, until sugar dissolves. Sprinkle gelatine over the remaining water in small jug; stir into milk mixture until gelatine dissolves. Cool. Beat butter and extract in small bowl with electric mixer until as white as possible. Gradually beat in milk mixture until light and fluffy.

prep + cook time 55 minutes (+ refrigeration & cooling)
makes 24

little cakes

madeleines

2 eggs
2 tablespoons caster (superfine) sugar
2 tablespoons icing (confectioners') sugar
1 teaspoon vanilla extract
¼ cup (35g) self-raising flour
¼ cup (35g) plain (all-purpose) flour
75g (2½ ounces) butter, melted
1 tablespoon hot water
2 tablespoons icing (confectioners') sugar, extra

1 Preheat oven to 200°C/400°F. Grease two 12-hole (1½-tablespoon/30ml) madeleine pans with a little butter.
2 Beat eggs, caster sugar, icing sugar and extract in small bowl with electric mixer until thick and creamy.
3 Meanwhile, sift flours twice. Sift flours over egg mixture; pour combined butter and the water down side of bowl then fold ingredients together.
4 Drop rounded tablespoons of mixture into pan holes.
5 Bake madeleines about 10 minutes. Tap hot pan firmly on bench to release madeleines then turn immediately onto baking-paper-covered wire racks to cool. Serve dusted with extra sifted icing sugar.

prep + cook time 25 minutes
makes 24

little cakes

carrot cakes

⅓ cup (80ml) vegetable oil
½ cup (110g) firmly packed light brown sugar
1 egg
1 cup firmly packed, coarsely grated carrot
⅓ cup (40g) finely chopped walnuts
¾ cup (110g) self-raising flour
½ teaspoon mixed spice
1 tablespoon pepitas, chopped finely
1 tablespoon finely chopped dried apricots
1 tablespoon finely chopped walnuts, extra

lemon cream cheese frosting
90g (3 ounces) cream cheese, softened
30g (1 ounce) unsalted butter, softened
1 teaspoon finely grated lemon rind
1½ cups (240g) icing (confectioners') sugar

1 Preheat oven to 180°C/350°F. Line 18 holes of two 12-hole (2-tablespoon/40ml) deep flat-based patty pans with paper cases.
2 Beat oil, sugar and egg in small bowl with electric mixer until thick and creamy. Stir in carrot and nuts, then sifted flour and spice. Divide mixture into paper cases.
3 Bake cakes about 20 minutes. Stand cakes 5 minutes before turning top-side up onto wire rack to cool.
4 Meanwhile, make lemon cream cheese frosting.
5 Spoon lemon cream cheese frosting into piping bag fitted with 2cm (¾-inch) fluted tube; pipe frosting onto cakes. Sprinkle cakes with combined pepitas, apricots and extra nuts.

lemon cream cheese frosting
Beat cream cheese, butter and rind in small bowl with electric mixer until light and fluffy; gradually beat in sifted icing sugar.

prep + cook time
45 minutes (+ cooling)
makes 18

black forest gateaux

It is fine to use just one 300ml carton of thickened cream for this recipe.

185g (6 ounces) unsalted butter, softened
1½ cups (330g) caster (superfine) sugar
6 eggs, separated
¾ cup (110g) self-raising flour
⅔ cup (70g) cocoa powder
2 tablespoons milk
½ cup (125ml) blackcurrant liqueur or cherry brandy
1 cup (320g) black cherry jam
1¼ cups (310ml) thickened (heavy) cream, whipped
1 cup (200g) seeded drained sour cherries, halved

chocolate ganache
½ cup (125ml) pouring cream
220g (7 ounces) dark eating (semi-sweet) chocolate, chopped coarsely

1 Preheat oven to 180°C/350°F. Grease 20cm x 30cm (8-inch x 12-inch) lamington pan; line with baking paper, extending paper 5cm (2 inches) over long sides.
2 Beat butter, sugar and egg yolks in small bowl with electric mixer until light and fluffy. Stir in sifted flour and cocoa and milk, in two batches.
3 Beat egg whites in clean small bowl with electric mixer until soft peaks form. Fold egg whites into cake mixture, in two batches. Spread mixture into pan.
4 Bake cake about 35 minutes. Stand cake 5 minutes before turning top-side up onto wire rack to cool.
5 Meanwhile, make chocolate ganache.
6 Trim edges from all sides of cake; cut cake into 40 squares. Split each square in half; brush each half with liqueur. Sandwich cakes with jam and cream; top with chocolate ganache and cherries.

chocolate ganache Bring cream to the boil in small saucepan. Remove from heat; pour over chocolate in small bowl, stir until smooth. Stand at room temperature until thickened slightly.

prep + cook time
1 hour 15 minutes (+ cooling)
makes 40

apple cinnamon tea loaves

90g (3 ounces) butter, softened
1 teaspoon vanilla extract
½ cup (110g) caster (superfine) sugar
1 egg
1⅓ cups (200g) self-raising flour
½ cup (125ml) milk
1 medium red apple (150g), quartered, cored, sliced thinly
15g (½ ounce) butter, melted
1 tablespoon white (granulated) sugar
½ teaspoon ground cinnamon
spiced honey cream
⅔ cup (160ml) double (thick) cream
2 teaspoons honey
¼ teaspoon ground ginger
pinch ground cinnamon

1 Preheat oven to 180°C/350°F. Grease 8-hole (¾-cup/180ml) petite loaf pan.
2 Beat softened butter, extract and caster sugar in small bowl with electric mixer until light and fluffy. Add egg, beat until combined. Stir in sifted flour and milk, in two batches.
3 Divide mixture into pan holes; top with apple, brush with melted butter, sprinkle with half the combined white sugar and cinnamon.
4 Bake loaves about 20 minutes. Sprinkle hot loaves with remaining sugar and cinnamon mixture. Stand loaves 5 minutes before turning top-side up onto wire rack to cool.
5 Meanwhile, make spiced honey cream.
6 Serve warm cakes with spiced honey cream.
spiced honey cream Combine ingredients in small bowl.

prep + cook time 35 minutes
makes 8

mini chocolate hazelnut cakes

100g (3 ounces) dark eating (semi-sweet) chocolate, chopped coarsely
¾ cup (180ml) water
100g (3 ounces) butter, softened
1 cup (220g) firmly packed light brown sugar
3 eggs
¼ cup (25g) cocoa powder
¾ cup (110g) self-raising flour
⅓ cup (35g) ground hazelnuts

whipped hazelnut ganache
⅓ cup (80ml) thickened (heavy) cream
185g (6 ounces) milk eating chocolate, chopped finely
2 tablespoons hazelnut-flavoured liqueur

1 Preheat oven to 180°C/350°F. Grease 12-hole (½-cup/125ml) oval friand pan.
2 Make whipped hazelnut ganache.
3 Meanwhile, combine chocolate and the water in medium saucepan; stir over low heat until smooth.
4 Beat butter and sugar in small bowl with electric mixer until light and fluffy. Add eggs, one at a time, beating until just combined between additions (mixture might separate at this stage, but will come together later); transfer mixture to medium bowl. Stir in warm chocolate mixture, sifted cocoa and flour, and ground hazelnuts. Divide mixture into pan holes.
5 Bake cakes about 20 minutes. Stand cakes 5 minutes; turn, top-sides up, onto wire rack to cool. Spread ganache over cakes.

whipped hazelnut ganache
Combine cream and chocolate in small saucepan; stir over low heat until smooth. Stir in liqueur; transfer mixture to small bowl. Cover; stand about 2 hours or until just firm. Beat ganache in small bowl with electric mixer until mixture changes to a pale brown colour.

prep + cook time 1 hour (+ standing) makes 12

little cakes

rhubarb and almond cakes

These days, rhubarb is available all year. Be sure to discard every bit of the vegetable's leaf and use only the thinnest stalks (the thick ones tend to be stringy).

½ cup (125ml) milk
¼ cup (40g) blanched almonds, roasted
80g (2½ ounces) butter, softened
1 teaspoon vanilla extract
½ cup (110g) caster (superfine) sugar
2 eggs
1 cup (150g) self-raising flour

poached rhubarb
250g (8 ounces) trimmed rhubarb, chopped coarsely
¼ cup (60ml) water
½ cup (110g) white (granulated) sugar

1 Preheat oven to 180°C/350°F. Grease a 6-hole texas (¾-cup/180ml) muffin pan.
2 Make poached rhubarb.
3 Meanwhile, blend or process milk and nuts until smooth.
4 Beat butter, extract and sugar in small bowl with electric mixer until light and fluffy. Add eggs, one at a time, beating until just combined between additions (mixture might separate at this stage, but will come together later); transfer to large bowl. Stir in sifted flour and almond mixture. Divide mixture into pan holes.
5 Bake cakes 10 minutes. Carefully remove muffin pan from oven; divide drained rhubarb over muffins, bake further 15 minutes.
6 Stand muffins 5 minutes; turn, top-side up, onto wire rack to cool. Serve warm or cold with rhubarb syrup.
poached rhubarb Place ingredients in medium saucepan; bring to the boil. Reduce heat; simmer, uncovered, about 10 minutes or until rhubarb is just tender. Drain rhubarb over medium bowl; reserve rhubarb and syrup separately.

prep + cook time 1 hour
makes 6

passionfruit curd sponge cakes

You need four passionfruit to get the required amount of passionfruit pulp needed for this recipe.

3 eggs
½ cup (110g) caster (superfine) sugar
¾ cup (110g) self-raising flour
20g (¾ ounce) butter
¼ cup (60ml) boiling water

passionfruit curd
⅓ cup (80ml) passionfruit pulp
½ cup (110g) caster (superfine) sugar
2 eggs, beaten lightly
125g (4 ounces) unsalted butter, chopped coarsely

1 Make passionfruit curd.
2 Preheat oven to 180°C/350°F. Grease 12-hole (½-cup/125ml) oval friand pan with softened butter; dust lightly with flour.
3 Beat eggs in small bowl with electric mixer until thick and creamy. Gradually add sugar, beating until dissolved between additions. Transfer mixture to large bowl. Fold in sifted flour then combined butter and the boiling water. Divide mixture into pan holes.
4 Bake cakes about 12 minutes. Working quickly, loosen edges of cakes from pan using a small knife; turn immediately onto baking-paper-covered wire racks to cool.
5 Split cooled cakes in half. Spread cut-sides with curd; replace tops. Serve lightly dusted with a little sifted icing (confectioners') sugar.

passionfruit curd Stir ingredients in medium heatproof bowl over pan of simmering water about 10 minutes or until mixture coats the back of a wooden spoon. Cover; refrigerate 3 hours.

prep + cook time 40 minutes
(+ refrigeration & cooling)
makes 12

little cakes

gluten-free berry cupcakes

125g (4 ounces) butter, softened
2 teaspoons finely grated lemon rind
¾ cup (165g) caster (superfine) sugar
4 eggs
2 cups (240g) ground almonds
½ cup (40g) desiccated coconut
½ cup (100g) rice flour
1 teaspoon bicarbonate of soda (baking soda)
1 cup (150g) frozen mixed berries
1 tablespoon desiccated coconut, extra

1 Preheat oven to 180°C/350°F. Line 12-hole (⅓-cup/80ml) muffin pan with paper cases.

2 Beat butter, rind and sugar in small bowl with electric mixer until light and fluffy. Add eggs, one at a time, beating until just combined between additions (mixture will separate at this stage, but will come together later); transfer to large bowl. Stir in ground almonds, coconut, sifted flour and soda, then the berries. Divide mixture into paper cases.

3 Bake cakes about 25 minutes. Stand cupcakes 5 minutes; turn, top-sides up, onto wire rack to cool. Sprinkle with extra coconut.

prep + cook time 45 minutes
makes 12

ginger powder puffs with orange cream

2 eggs
⅓ cup (75g) caster (superfine) sugar
2 tablespoons cornflour (cornstarch)
1 tablespoon plain (all-purpose) flour
2 tablespoons self-raising flour
1 teaspoon cocoa powder
1½ teaspoons ground ginger
¼ teaspoon ground cinnamon

orange cream
⅔ cup (160ml) thickened (heavy) cream
2 tablespoons icing (confectioners') sugar
1 teaspoon finely grated orange rind

1 Preheat oven to 180°C/350°F. Grease and flour two 12-hole (1½-tablespoon/30ml) shallow round-based patty pans.
2 Beat eggs and sugar in small bowl with electric mixer until thick and creamy. Fold in triple-sifted dry ingredients. Divide mixture into pan holes.
3 Bake about 8 minutes. Working quickly, loosen edges of cakes using palette knife, then turn immediately onto baking-paper-covered wire racks to cool.
4 Meanwhile, make orange cream.
5 Just before serving, sandwich puffs together with orange cream. Serve lightly dusted with a little sifted icing sugar.
orange cream Beat cream and sifted icing sugar in small bowl with electric mixer until firm peaks form; fold in rind.

prep + cook time 35 minutes
makes 12

little cakes

jelly cakes with berry cream

It is fine to use just one 300ml carton of cream for this recipe.

125g (4 ounces) unsalted butter, softened
½ cup (110g) caster (superfine) sugar
2 teaspoons vanilla extract
2 eggs
1½ cups (225g) self-raising flour
⅓ cup (80ml) milk
2 cups (160g) desiccated coconut
1¼ cups (310ml) thickened (heavy) cream, whipped
1 tablespoon icing (confectioners') sugar
1 cup (150g) frozen mixed berries, chopped coarsely
25 fresh raspberries

mixed berry jelly
1 cup (150g) frozen mixed berries, thawed
1½ cups (375ml) apple blackcurrant juice
⅓ cup (75g) caster (superfine) sugar
¼ cup (60ml) water
3 teaspoons gelatine

1 Preheat oven to 180°C/350°F. Grease 22cm (9-inch) square cake pan well with butter; line base with baking paper.
2 Beat butter, caster sugar and half the extract in small bowl with electric mixer until light and fluffy. Beat in eggs, one at a time. Stir in sifted flour and milk, in two batches. Spread mixture into pan.
3 Bake cake about 25 minutes. Stand cake 5 minutes before turning top-side up onto wire rack to cool.
4 Meanwhile, make mixed berry jelly.
5 Trim edges from all sides of cake; cut cake into 25 squares. Dip each square into jelly then roll in coconut. Place on tray, cover; refrigerate 30 minutes.
6 Beat cream, icing sugar and remaining extract in small bowl with electric mixer until soft peaks form; fold in berries. Split each jelly cake in half; sandwich with berry cream. Top each jelly cake with a fresh raspberry.

mixed berry jelly Blend or process berries until smooth. Stir juice, sugar and berry puree in medium saucepan over medium heat until sugar dissolves. Strain mixture through fine sieve; discard solids. Place the water in small heatproof jug; sprinkle over gelatine. Stand jug in small saucepan of simmering water, stirring, until gelatine dissolves. Stir gelatine mixture into berry mixture. Pour into shallow dish; refrigerate, stirring occasionally, until set to the consistency of unbeaten egg white.

prep + cook time
1 hour 10 minutes (+ refrigeration)
makes 25

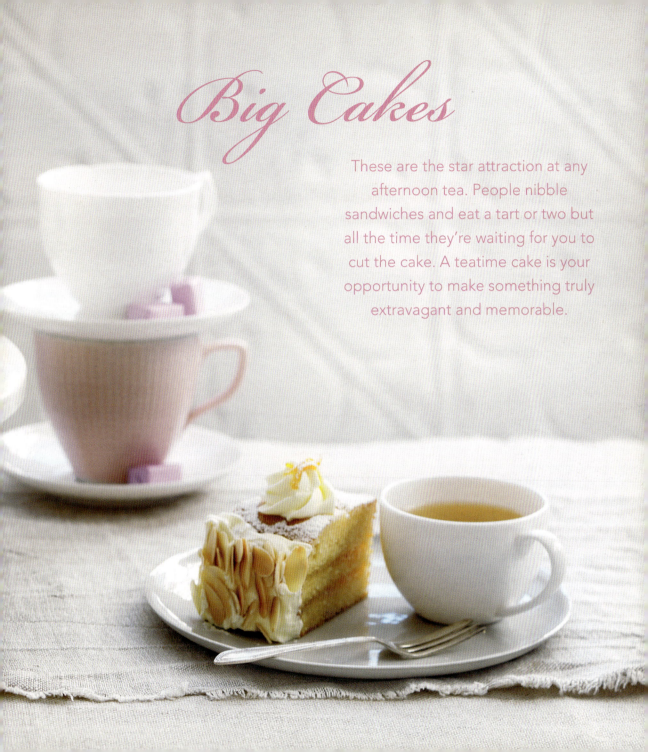

Big Cakes

These are the star attraction at any afternoon tea. People nibble sandwiches and eat a tart or two but all the time they're waiting for you to cut the cake. A teatime cake is your opportunity to make something truly extravagant and memorable.

pink velvet cake

It is fine to use just one 300ml carton of thickened cream for this recipe.

125g (4 ounces) butter, softened
1 teaspoon vanilla extract
1½ cups (330g) caster (superfine) sugar
2 eggs
1½ cups (225g) plain (all-purpose) flour
2 tablespoons cornflour (cornstarch)
2 tablespoons cocoa powder
1 cup (250ml) buttermilk
1 tablespoon rose pink food colouring
1 teaspoon white vinegar
1 teaspoon bicarbonate of soda (baking soda)
1 cup (50g) flaked coconut

mascarpone frosting
250g (8 ounces) cream cheese, softened
250g (8 ounces) mascarpone cheese
1 cup (160g) icing (confectioners') sugar
1 teaspoon vanilla extract
1¼ cups (310ml) thickened (heavy) cream

1 Preheat oven to 180°C/350°F. Grease two deep 23cm (9-inch) round cake pans; line bases and sides with baking paper.
2 Beat butter, extract, sugar and eggs in small bowl with electric mixer until light and fluffy. Transfer mixture to large bowl; stir in sifted flours and cocoa and combined buttermilk and food colouring, in two batches.
3 Combine vinegar and soda in a cup; allow to fizz then fold into cake mixture. Divide mixture between pans.
4 Bake cakes about 25 minutes. Stand cakes 10 minutes before turning top-side up onto wire racks to cool. Enclose cakes in plastic wrap; freeze 40 minutes.
5 Meanwhile, make mascarpone frosting.
6 Split cold cakes in half. Place one layer on serving plate, cut-side up; spread with ⅔ cup frosting. Repeat layering, finishing with remaining frosting spread over top and side of cake; press coconut onto side of cake.

mascarpone frosting Beat cream cheese, mascarpone, sugar and extract in small bowl with electric mixer until smooth. Beat in cream.

prep + cook time
1 hour (+ cooling & freezing)
serves 12

orange almond victoria sponge

It is fine to use just one 300ml carton of thickened cream for this recipe.

185g (6 ounces) unsalted butter, softened
1 teaspoon vanilla extract
¾ cup (165g) caster (superfine) sugar
3 eggs
¼ cup (60ml) milk
1½ cups (225g) self-raising flour
1 cup (320g) orange marmalade, warmed
1¼ cups (310ml) thickened (heavy) cream
2 tablespoons icing (confectioners') sugar
½ cup (40g) flaked almonds, roasted

1 Preheat oven to 180°C/350°F. Grease deep 20cm (8-inch) ring pan well with butter.
2 Beat butter, extract, and caster sugar in small bowl with electric mixer until light and fluffy. Beat in eggs, one at a time. Stir in milk and sifted flour, in two batches. Spread mixture into pan.
3 Bake sponge about 30 minutes. Turn sponge immediately onto baking-paper-covered wire rack, turn top-side up to cool.
4 Meanwhile, strain marmalade through fine sieve; reserve syrup and rind separately.
5 Beat cream and half the icing sugar in small bowl with electric mixer until soft peaks form.
6 Split sponge into three layers. Place one layer onto serving plate, cut-side up; spread with half of the marmalade syrup. Top with another layer of sponge and remaining syrup; top with remaining layer of sponge. Cut sponge into twelve pieces, keeping cake in ring shape.
7 Spread two-thirds of the cream around side of sponge; press almonds into cream. Spoon remaining cream into piping bag fitted with 1cm (½-inch) fluted tube. Pipe rosettes on top of cake; top with some of the reserved rind. Serve sponge dusted with remaining icing sugar.

prep + cook time
55 minutes (+ cooling)
serves 12

chocolate and pecan torte

If you can't find ground pecans, simply blend or process 150g (4½ ounces) of roasted pecans until they are finely ground. Be sure to use the pulse button, however, because you want to achieve a flour-like texture, not a paste.

200g (6½ ounces) dark eating (semi-sweet) chocolate, chopped coarsely
150g (4½ ounces) butter, chopped coarsely
5 eggs, separated
¾ cup (165g) caster (superfine) sugar
1½ cups (150g) ground pecans
ganache
½ cup (125ml) pouring cream
200g (6½ ounces) dark eating (semi-sweet) chocolate, chopped coarsely

1 Preheat oven to 180°C/350°F. Grease deep 22cm (9-inch) round cake pan; line base and side with baking paper.
2 Stir chocolate and butter in small saucepan over low heat until smooth; cool 10 minutes.
3 Beat egg yolks and sugar in small bowl with electric mixer until thick and creamy. Transfer to large bowl; fold in chocolate mixture and ground pecans.
4 Beat egg whites in small bowl with electric mixer until soft peaks form; fold into chocolate mixture, in two batches. Pour mixture into pan.
5 Bake cake about 55 minutes. Stand cake 15 minutes; turn, top-side up, onto baking-paper-covered wire rack to cool.
6 Meanwhile, make ganache.
7 Pour ganache over cake; refrigerate cake 30 minutes before serving.
ganache Bring cream to the boil in small saucepan. Remove from heat; add chocolate, stir until smooth.

prep + cook time
1 hour 20 minutes
(+ standing & refrigeration)
serves 8

raspberry cream sponge

Use a serrated or electric knife to split and cut the sponge.

4 eggs
¾ cup (165g) caster (superfine) sugar
⅔ cup (100g) wheaten cornflour (cornstarch)
¼ cup (30g) custard powder
1 teaspoon cream of tartar
½ teaspoon bicarbonate of soda (baking soda)
¾ cup (240g) raspberry jam
1½ cups (375ml) thickened (heavy) cream, whipped

raspberry glacé icing
45g (1½ ounces) fresh raspberries
2 cups (320g) icing (confectioners') sugar
15g (½ ounce) butter, softened
2 teaspoons hot water, approximately

1 Preheat oven to 180°C/350°F. Grease deep 22cm (9-inch) square cake pan with butter.
2 Beat eggs and sugar in small bowl with electric mixer about 10 minutes or until thick and creamy and sugar has dissolved; transfer to large bowl.
3 Sift dry ingredients twice, then sift over egg mixture; fold dry ingredients into egg mixture. Spread mixture into pan.
4 Bake sponge about 25 minutes. Turn sponge immediately onto baking-paper-covered wire rack, then turn top-side up to cool.
5 Meanwhile, make raspberry glacé icing.
6 Split sponge in half. Sandwich with jam and cream. Spread sponge with icing, sprinkle with fresh rose petals.

raspberry glacé icing Push raspberries through fine sieve into small heatproof bowl; discard solids. Sift icing sugar into same bowl; stir in butter and enough of the water to make a thick paste. Place bowl over small saucepan of simmering water; stir until icing is spreadable.

prep + cook time
50 minutes (+ cooling)
serves 16

pistachio buttercake with orange honey syrup

Unless stated otherwise, use roasted unsalted nuts when making a cake. Buy the freshest nuts you can: they should taste slightly sweet.

2 cups (280g) roasted unsalted pistachios, chopped coarsely
185g (6 ounces) butter, softened
1 tablespoon finely grated orange rind
¾ cup (165g) caster (superfine) sugar
3 eggs
¼ cup (60ml) buttermilk
1½ cups (225g) self-raising flour
¾ cup (110g) plain (all-purpose) flour

orange honey syrup
1 cup (220g) caster (superfine) sugar
1 cup (250ml) water
1 tablespoon honey
1 cinnamon stick
1 teaspoon cardamom seeds
3 star anise
3 strips orange rind

1 Make orange honey syrup; cool.
2 Preheat oven to 180°C/350°F. Grease 22cm (9-inch) square slab cake pan; line base and sides with baking paper, extending paper 2.5cm (1 inch) over sides. Sprinkle nuts over base of pan.
3 Beat butter, rind and sugar in small bowl with electric mixer until light and fluffy. Add eggs, one at a time, beating until just combined between additions; transfer mixture to large bowl. Stir in combined buttermilk and ⅓ cup of the orange honey syrup, and sifted flours, in two batches. Spread mixture into pan.
4 Bake cake about 40 minutes. Stand cake 5 minutes; turn, top-side up, onto baking-paper-covered wire rack. Brush surface of hot cake with half of the remaining heated syrup.
5 Cut cake into squares, serve warm, drizzled with remaining heated syrup.

orange honey syrup Stir ingredients in small saucepan over low heat, without boiling, until sugar dissolves; bring to the boil. Remove from heat; cool 15 minutes then strain.

prep + cook time
1 hour 10 minutes
serves 16

lime and poppy seed syrup cake

Before grating the lime, make sure it is at room temperature and roll it, pressing down hard with your hand, on the kitchen bench. This will help extract as much juice as possible from the fruit. You can substitute the same weight of other citrus fruit – lemons, mandarins, oranges, blood oranges etc – for the limes if you wish.

¼ cup (40g) poppy seeds
½ cup (125ml) milk
250g (8 ounces) butter, softened
1 tablespoon finely grated lime rind
1¼ cups (275g) caster (superfine) sugar
4 eggs
2¼ cups (335g) self-raising flour
¾ cup (110g) plain (all-purpose) flour
1 cup (240g) sour cream

lime syrup
½ cup (125ml) lime juice
1 cup (250ml) water
1 cup (220g) caster (superfine) sugar

1 Preheat oven to 180°C/350°F. Grease base and sides of deep 22cm (9-inch) square cake pan.
2 Combine poppy seeds and milk in small jug; soak 10 minutes.
3 Beat butter, rind and sugar in small bowl with electric mixer until light and fluffy. Add eggs, one at a time, beating until combined between additions; transfer mixture to large bowl. Stir in sifted flours, sour cream and poppy seed mixture, in two batches. Spread mixture into pan.
4 Bake cake about 1 hour.
5 Meanwhile, make lime syrup.
6 Stand cake 5 minutes, turn onto wire rack over tray. Pour hot lime syrup over hot cake.

lime syrup Stir ingredients in small saucepan over heat, without boiling, until sugar dissolves. Simmer, uncovered, without stirring, 5 minutes.

prep + cook time
1 hour 20 minutes
serves 16

tiramisu roulade

Use any coffee-flavoured liqueur you prefer in the mascarpone cream filling – you could also use chocolate, almond or hazelnut liqueur. This roulade uses plain rather than self-raising flour; its rising is thanks to the air incorporated into the eggs.

¼ cup (60ml) water
2 tablespoons coffee-flavoured liqueur
2 tablespoons caster (superfine) sugar
1 tablespoon instant coffee granules
1 tablespoon boiling water
3 eggs
½ cup (110g) caster (superfine) sugar, extra
½ cup (75g) plain (all-purpose) flour
2 tablespoons flaked almonds
2 teaspoons caster (superfine) sugar, extra

coffee liqueur cream
1 cup (250g) mascarpone cheese
½ cup (125ml) thickened (heavy) cream
2 tablespoons coffee-flavoured liqueur

1 Preheat oven to 220°C/425°F. Grease 25cm x 30cm (10-inch x 16-inch) swiss roll pan; line base and two long sides with baking paper, extending paper 5cm (2 inches) over long sides.
2 Bring the water, liqueur and sugar to the boil in small saucepan. Reduce heat; simmer, uncovered, without stirring, about 5 minutes or until syrup thickens slightly. Remove from heat, stir in half the coffee; reserve syrup.
3 Dissolve remaining coffee in the boiling water.
4 Beat eggs and extra sugar in small bowl with electric mixer about 5 minutes or until sugar is dissolved and mixture is thick; transfer to large bowl, fold in dissolved coffee.
5 Sift flour twice onto paper. Sift flour over egg mixture then fold gently into mixture. Spread sponge mixture into pan; sprinkle with nuts.
6 Bake sponge about 15 minutes.
7 Meanwhile, place a piece of baking paper cut the same size as swiss roll pan on bench; sprinkle evenly with a little more caster sugar. Turn sponge onto sugared paper; peel away lining paper. Use serrated knife to cut crisp edges from all sides of sponge. Roll sponge from long side, using paper as guide; cool.
8 Meanwhile, make coffee liqueur cream.
9 Unroll sponge, brush with reserved syrup. Spread cream over sponge then re-roll sponge. Cover with plastic wrap; refrigerate 30 minutes before serving.
coffee liqueur cream Beat ingredients in small bowl with electric mixer until firm peaks form.

prep + cook time
55 minutes (+ refrigeration)
serves 8

berry cream roulade

3 eggs
½ cup (110g) caster (superfine) sugar
½ cup (75g) wheaten cornflour
1 tablespoon custard powder
1 teaspoon cream of tartar
½ teaspoon bicarbonate of soda (baking soda)
1 tablespoon caster (superfine) sugar, extra
1 tablespoon icing (confectioners') sugar

berry cream
¾ cup (180ml) thickened (heavy) cream
1 teaspoon vanilla extract
1 tablespoon icing (confectioners') sugar
1 cup (150g) frozen blackberries, chopped coarsely

1 Preheat oven to 180°C/350°F. Grease 25cm x 30cm (10-inch x 12-inch) swiss roll pan; line base and two long sides with baking paper, extending paper 5cm (2 inches) over long sides.
2 Beat eggs and caster sugar in small bowl with electric mixer about 5 minutes or until sugar is dissolved and mixture is thick and creamy; transfer to large bowl.
3 Sift cornflour, custard powder, cream of tartar and soda together twice onto paper then sift over egg mixture; gently fold dry ingredients into egg mixture. Spread sponge mixture into pan.
4 Bake sponge about 12 minutes.
5 Meanwhile, place a piece of baking paper cut the same size as swiss roll pan on bench; sprinkle evenly with extra caster sugar. Turn sponge onto sugared paper; peel away lining paper. Use serrated knife to cut away crisp edges from all sides of sponge. Roll sponge from long side, using paper as a guide; cover with a tea towel, then cool.
6 Meanwhile, make berry cream.
7 Unroll sponge, spread cream over sponge then re-roll sponge. Dust with sifted icing sugar.

berry cream Beat cream, extract and icing sugar in small bowl with electric mixer until soft peaks form; fold in thawed berries.

prep + cook time 30 minutes
serves 8

lemon and lime white chocolate mud cake

Grate the citrus rind called for here then save the fruit to extract the juice for another use. Without this protective "skin", the fruit will become dry and hard, so they should be juiced, say for a salsa or salad dressing, within a day or two.

250g (8 ounces) butter, chopped
2 teaspoons each finely grated lemon rind and lime rind
180g (5½ ounces) white eating chocolate, chopped coarsely
1½ cups (330g) caster (superfine) sugar
¾ cup (180ml) milk
1½ cups (225g) plain (all-purpose) flour
½ cup (75g) self-raising flour
2 eggs, beaten lightly

coconut ganache
360g (11½ ounces) white eating chocolate, chopped finely
1 teaspoon each finely grated lemon rind and lime rind
½ cup (125ml) coconut cream

1 Preheat oven to 170°C/340°F. Grease deep 20cm (8-inch) round cake pan; line base with baking paper.
2 Stir butter, rinds, chocolate, sugar and milk in medium saucepan over low heat until smooth. Transfer mixture to large bowl; cool 15 minutes.
3 Stir in sifted flours and egg; pour mixture into pan.
4 Bake about 1 hour 40 minutes; cool cake in pan.
5 Meanwhile, make coconut ganache.
6 Turn cake, top-side up, onto serving plate; spread ganache over cake.

coconut ganache Combine chocolate and rinds in medium bowl. Bring coconut cream to the boil in small saucepan; pour over chocolate mixture, stir until smooth. Cover bowl; refrigerate, stirring occasionally, about 30 minutes or until ganache is spreadable.

prep + cook time
2 hours 20 minutes
(+ cooling & refrigeration)
serves 10

chocolate banana cake

You will need about 2 large overripe bananas (460g) for this recipe. It is very important that the bananas you use are overripe; less-ripe ones won't mash easily and cause the cake to be too heavy.

⅔ cup (160ml) milk
2 teaspoons lemon juice
150g (4½ ounces) butter, softened
1 cup (220g) caster (superfine) sugar
2 eggs
2 cups (300g) self-raising flour
½ teaspoon bicarbonate of soda (baking soda)
1 cup mashed banana
100g (3 ounces) dark eating (semi-sweet) chocolate, grated finely

creamy choc frosting
200g (6½ ounces) dark eating (semi-sweet) chocolate, chopped coarsely
1 cup (160g) icing (confectioners') sugar
½ cup (120g) sour cream

1 Preheat oven to 170°C/340°F. Grease deep 22cm (9-inch) round cake pan; line base with baking paper.
2 Combine milk and juice in small jug; stand 10 minutes.
3 Meanwhile, beat butter and sugar in small bowl with electric mixer until light and fluffy. Beat in eggs, one at a time; transfer mixture to large bowl. Stir in sifted flour and soda, banana, milk mixture and chocolate.
4 Spread mixture into pan; bake about 1 hour 10 minutes. Stand cake 5 minutes before turning, top-side up, onto wire rack to cool.
5 Meanwhile, make creamy choc frosting. Spread cold cake with frosting.

creamy choc frosting Melt chocolate in medium heatproof bowl over medium saucepan of simmering water; gradually stir in sifted icing sugar and sour cream.

prep + cook time
1 hour 30 minutes
serves 10

big cakes

brown sugar sponge

It is fine to use just one 300ml carton of cream for this recipe. Filled sponge is best eaten the day it is made. Unfilled sponge can be frozen for up to 2 months.

4 eggs
¾ cup (165g) firmly packed dark brown sugar
1 cup (150g) wheaten cornflour (cornstarch)
1 teaspoon cream of tartar
½ teaspoon bicarbonate of soda (baking soda)
1¼ cups (310ml) thickened (heavy) cream

praline
⅓ cup (75g) white (granulated) sugar
¼ cup (60ml) water
½ teaspoon malt vinegar
⅓ cup (45g) roasted hazelnuts

1 Preheat oven to 180°C/350°F. Grease two deep 22cm (9-inch) round cake pans.
2 Beat eggs and brown sugar in small bowl with electric mixer about 10 minutes or until thick and creamy; transfer to large bowl.
3 Sift cornflour, cream of tartar and soda twice onto paper then sift over egg mixture; gently fold dry ingredients into egg mixture. Divide mixture between pans.
4 Bake cakes about 18 minutes. Turn immediately onto baking-paper-covered wire racks to cool.
5 Meanwhile, make praline.
6 Beat cream in small bowl with electric mixer until firm peaks form; fold in praline. Place one sponge on serving plate; spread with half the cream mixture. Top with remaining sponge; spread with remaining cream mixture.

praline Stir sugar, the water and vinegar in small saucepan over heat, without boiling, until sugar dissolves; bring to the boil. Reduce heat; simmer, uncovered, without stirring, about 10 minutes or until syrup is golden brown. Add hazelnuts; pour praline mixture onto baking-paper-lined tray. Cool about 15 minutes or until set. Break praline into pieces then blend or process until mixture is as fine (or as coarse) as desired.

prep + cook time
50 minutes (+ cooling)
serves 8

fresh ginger cake with golden ginger cream

It is fine to use just one 300ml carton of cream in the golden ginger cream recipe.

250g (8 ounces) butter, chopped
½ cup (110g) firmly packed light brown sugar
⅔ cup (230g) golden syrup or treacle
12cm (4¾-inch) piece fresh ginger (60g), grated finely
1 cup (150g) plain (all-purpose) flour
1 cup (150g) self-raising flour
½ teaspoon bicarbonate of soda (baking soda)
2 eggs, beaten lightly
¾ cup (180ml) thickened (heavy) cream

golden ginger cream
1¼ cups (310ml) thickened (heavy) cream
2 tablespoons golden syrup or treacle
2 teaspoons ground ginger

1 Preheat oven to 180°C/350°F. Grease deep 22cm (9-inch) round cake pan.
2 Melt butter in medium saucepan, add sugar, syrup and ginger; stir over low heat until sugar dissolves.
3 Whisk in combined sifted flours and soda then egg and cream. Pour mixture into pan.
4 Bake cake about 50 minutes. Stand cake 10 minutes; turn, top-side up, onto wire rack to cool.
5 Meanwhile, make golden ginger cream.
6 Serve cake with cream.
golden ginger cream Beat ingredients in small bowl with electric mixer until soft peaks form.

prep + cook time
1 hour 15 minutes
serves 10

big cakes

lemon cake

Grate the lemon for the frosting before you extract the juice for the cake mixture. Frosted cake will keep in an airtight container, in the fridge, for up to 3 days.

125g (4 ounces) butter, softened
2 teaspoons finely grated lemon rind
1¼ cups (275g) caster (superfine) sugar
3 eggs
1½ cups (225g) self-raising flour
½ cup (125ml) milk
¼ cup (60ml) lemon juice

lemon mascarpone frosting
1 cup (250ml) thickened (heavy) cream
½ cup (80g) icing (confectioners') sugar
2 teaspoons finely grated lemon rind
⅔ cup (170g) mascarpone cheese

1 Preheat oven to 180°C/350°F. Grease deep 20cm (8-inch) round cake pan; line base with baking paper.
2 Make lemon mascarpone frosting. Refrigerate, covered, until required.
3 Beat butter, rind and sugar in small bowl with electric mixer until light and fluffy. Beat in eggs, one at a time (mixture might separate at this stage, but will come together later); transfer mixture to large bowl. Stir in sifted flour, milk and juice, in two batches. Pour mixture into pan.
4 Bake cake about 50 minutes. Stand cake in pan 5 minutes before turning, top-side up, onto wire rack to cool.
5 Split cold cake into three layers, place one layer onto serving plate, cut-side up; spread with one-third of the frosting. Repeat layering process, finishing with frosting.

lemon mascarpone frosting
Beat cream, sifted icing sugar and rind in small bowl with electric mixer until soft peaks form. Fold cream mixture into mascarpone.

prep + cook time
1 hour 20 minutes
serves 8

upside-down toffee date and banana cake

You will need 1 large overripe banana (230g) for the amount of mashed banana. It is important that the banana you use is overripe; less-ripe ones won't mash easily and can cause the cake to be too heavy. We prefer to use an underproof rum in baking. It is fine to use just one 300ml carton of cream for this recipe.

1½ cups (330g) caster (superfine) sugar
1½ cups (375ml) water
3 star anise
2 medium bananas (400g), sliced thinly
1 cup (140g) seeded dried dates
¾ cup (180ml) water, extra
½ cup (125ml) dark rum
1 teaspoon bicarbonate of soda (baking soda)
60g (2 ounces) butter, chopped
½ cup (110g) firmly packed light brown sugar
2 eggs
2 teaspoons mixed spice
1 cup (150g) self-raising flour
½ cup mashed banana
1¼ cups (310ml) thickened (heavy) cream

1 Preheat oven to 180°C/350°F. Grease deep 22cm (9-inch) round cake pan; line base with baking paper.
2 Stir caster sugar, the water and star anise in medium saucepan over low heat, without boiling, until sugar dissolves. Bring to the boil; boil syrup, uncovered, without stirring, about 5 minutes or until thickened slightly. Strain ½ cup of the syrup into small heatproof jug; reserve to flavour cream. Discard star-anise.
3 To make toffee, continue boiling remaining syrup, uncovered, without stirring, about 10 minutes or until toffee is golden brown. Pour hot toffee into cake pan; top with sliced banana.
4 Place dates, the extra water and rum in small saucepan; bring to the boil then remove from heat. Stir in soda; stand 5 minutes. Blend or process date mixture with butter and brown sugar until almost smooth. Add eggs, spice and flour; blend or process until just combined. Stir in mashed banana. Pour mixture into pan.
5 Bake cake about 40 minutes. Turn cake, in pan, onto serving plate; stand 2 minutes. Remove pan then baking paper.
6 To make star anise cream, beat cream in small bowl with electric mixer until firm peaks form. Stir in reserved syrup.
7 Serve cake warm or at room temperature with star anise cream.

prep + cook time
1 hour 30 minutes
serves 8

big cakes

spices of the orient teacake

The secret to a successful teacake lies in the beating of the sugar, egg and butter – the mixture must be very light in colour and full of air.

60g (2 ounces) butter, softened
1 teaspoon vanilla extract
½ cup (110g) caster (superfine) sugar
1 egg
1 cup (150g) self-raising flour
⅓ cup (80ml) milk
20g (¾ ounce) butter, melted, extra

spiced nuts
2 tablespoons shelled pistachios, chopped finely
2 tablespoons blanched almonds, chopped finely
2 tablespoons pine nuts, chopped finely
¼ cup (40g) icing (confectioners') sugar
1 teaspoon ground cinnamon
½ teaspoon each ground allspice and ground cardamom

1 Preheat oven to 180°C/350°F. Grease 20cm (8-inch) round cake pan.
2 Beat butter, extract, sugar and egg in small bowl with electric mixer until light and fluffy. Stir in sifted flour and milk. Spread mixture into pan.
3 Bake cake about 25 minutes. Stand cake 5 minutes; turn, top-side up, onto wire rack to cool.
4 Meanwhile, make spiced nuts.
5 Brush cooled cake with extra butter; sprinkle with spiced nuts. Serve warm.

spiced nuts Place nuts in strainer; rinse under cold water. Combine wet nuts in large bowl with icing sugar and spices; spread mixture onto oven tray, roast in oven about 10 minutes or until nuts are dry.

prep + cook time 45 minutes
serves 10

boiled whisky fruit cake

This rich fruit cake will keep indefinitely if stored in an airtight container in a clean cool, dark place, or in the fridge or freezer.

1½ cups (250g) raisins
1½ cups (210g) seeded dried dates
1½ cups (250g) seeded prunes
1½ cups (250g) sultanas
⅓ cup (70g) red glacé cherries, quartered
⅓ cup (55g) mixed peel
2 tablespoons caster (superfine) sugar
30g (1 ounce) butter
½ cup (125ml) whisky
250g (8 ounces) butter, chopped, extra
1 cup (220g) firmly packed dark brown sugar
½ teaspoon bicarbonate of soda (baking soda)
½ cup (70g) slivered almonds
2 cups (300g) plain (all-purpose) flour
2 teaspoons mixed spice
5 eggs
¼ cup (60ml) whisky, extra

1 Chop raisins, dates and prunes the same size as the sultanas (this will help make the finished cake cut better); combine in a large bowl with sultanas, cherries and peel.
2 Place caster sugar in large heavy-based saucepan over medium heat; turn pan occasionally until sugar is melted. Add butter and whisky; stir over low heat until smooth.
3 Add extra butter, brown sugar and fruit to pan. Stir over heat until butter melts; bring to the boil. Remove from heat; stir in soda. Transfer to large bowl, cover; stand overnight at room temperature.
4 Preheat oven to 150°C/300°F. Grease deep 20cm (8-inch) square cake pan; line base and sides with two layers of brown paper then baking paper, extending paper 5cm (2 inches) over sides.
5 Add nuts, sifted flour and spice, and eggs to fruit mixture; stir until well combined.
6 Spoon mixture into corners of pan then spread remaining mixture into pan. Drop pan from a height of about 15cm (6 inches) onto bench to settle mixture into pan and to break any large air bubbles; level surface of cake with wet spatula.
7 Bake cake about 3 hours. Brush hot cake with extra whisky. Cover hot cake tightly with foil; cool in pan.

prep + cook time
3 hours 35 minutes (+ standing)
serves 20

almond carrot cake

Store iced cake in an airtight container, in the fridge, for up to 4 days.

5 eggs, separated
1 teaspoon finely grated lemon rind
1¼ cups (275g) caster (superfine) sugar
2 cups (480g) coarsely grated carrot
2 cups (240g) ground almonds
½ cup (75g) self-raising flour
2 tablespoons roasted slivered almonds

cream cheese frosting
100g (3 ounces) cream cheese, softened
80g (2½ ounces) butter, softened
½ cup (80g) icing (confectioners') sugar
1 teaspoon lemon juice

1 Preheat oven to 180°C/350°F. Grease deep 20cm (8-inch) square cake pan; line base with baking paper.
2 Beat egg yolks, rind and sugar in small bowl with electric mixer until thick and creamy; transfer to large bowl. Stir in carrot, ground almonds and sifted flour.
3 Beat egg whites in small bowl with electric mixer until soft peaks form; fold into carrot mixture, in two batches. Pour mixture into pan.
4 Bake cake about 1¼ hours. Stand cake 5 minutes before turning, top-side up, onto wire rack to cool.
5 Meanwhile, make cream cheese frosting.
6 Spread cold cake with cream cheese frosting; sprinkle with slivered almonds.

cream cheese frosting Beat cream cheese and butter in small bowl with electric mixer until light and fluffy; gradually beat in sifted icing sugar and juice.

prep + cook time
1 hour 35 minutes
serves 10

muscat prune shortcake

It is fine to use just one 300ml carton of cream for this recipe. A fortified wine, like sherry and port, muscat is the result of grapes left to ripen well beyond normal harvesting time, resulting in a concentrated dark, toffee-coloured wine with a rich yet mellow flavour.

200g (6½ ounces) butter, softened
1 teaspoon finely grated lemon rind
⅓ cup (75g) caster (superfine) sugar
¼ cup (50g) rice flour
¾ cup (110g) self-raising flour
¾ cup (110g) plain (all-purpose) flour
1¼ cups (310ml) thickened (heavy) cream
1 tablespoon caster (superfine) sugar, extra

muscat prunes
1 cup (170g) seeded prunes, chopped coarsely
1 cup (250ml) muscat

1 Preheat oven to 180°C/350°F. Grease three 20cm (8-inch) round sandwich pans.
2 Beat butter, rind and sugar in medium bowl with electric mixer until light and fluffy. Fold in sifted flours, in two batches. Press mixture evenly into pans.
3 Bake shortcakes about 20 minutes. Stand shortcakes in pans; cool to room temperature.
4 Meanwhile, make muscat prunes.
5 Beat cream in small bowl with electric mixer until firm peaks form. Place one shortcake into deep 20cm (8-inch) round cake pan or 20cm (8-inch) springform tin; spread with half the prune mixture then half the whipped cream. Top with another shortcake; spread with remaining prune mixture then remaining whipped cream. Top with remaining shortcake, cover; refrigerate overnight.
6 Remove shortcake from pan; serve sprinkled with extra sugar.

muscat prunes Stir prunes and muscat in small saucepan over heat, without boiling, until prunes soften. Cool to room temperature.

prep + cook time 55 minutes (+ cooling & refrigeration) serves 12

big cakes

chocolate mud cake with chilli cherries

250g (8 ounces) butter, chopped
200g (6½ ounces) dark eating (semi-sweet) chocolate, chopped coarsely
2 cups (440g) caster (superfine) sugar
1 cup (250ml) milk
1 teaspoon vanilla extract
⅓ cup (80ml) bourbon
1½ cups (225g) plain (all-purpose) flour
¼ cup (35g) self-raising flour
¼ cup (25g) cocoa powder
2 eggs

chilli cherries
2 cups (500ml) water
¾ cup (165g) caster (superfine) sugar
1 fresh small red thai (serrano) chilli, halved lengthways
1 star anise
6 whole black peppercorns
10cm (4-inch) piece orange rind
300g (9½ ounces) frozen cherries

dark chocolate ganache
⅓ cup (80ml) pouring cream
200g (6½ ounces) dark eating (semi-sweet) chocolate, chopped coarsely

1 Preheat oven to 170°C/340°F. Grease deep 22cm (9-inch) round cake pan; line base with baking paper.
2 Combine butter, chocolate, sugar, milk, extract and bourbon in medium saucepan; stir over low heat until smooth. Transfer to large bowl; cool 15 minutes. Whisk in sifted flours and cocoa, then eggs. Pour mixture into pan.
3 Bake cake about 1½ hours.
4 Meanwhile, make chilli cherries.
5 Stand cake in pan 5 minutes; turn, top-side up, onto wire rack to cool.
6 Meanwhile, make dark chocolate ganache.
7 Spread ganache over top and side of cake; serve with chilli cherries.

chilli cherries Stir the water, sugar, chilli, star anise, peppercorns and rind in medium saucepan over low heat, without boiling, until sugar dissolves. Bring to the boil; boil 2 minutes. Add cherries; simmer 5 minutes or until cherries are just tender. Cool cherries in syrup. Remove cherries from pan; bring syrup to the boil. Boil 10 minutes or until syrup thickens slightly; cool. Return cherries to pan.
dark chocolate ganache Bring cream to the boil in small saucepan. Remove from heat; add chocolate, stir until smooth.

prep + cook time
1 hour 55 minutes (+ cooling)
serves 10

almond honey spice cake

125g (4 ounces) butter, softened
⅓ cup (75g) caster (superfine) sugar
2 tablespoons honey
1 teaspoon each ground ginger and ground allspice
2 eggs
1½ cups (180g) ground almonds
½ cup (80g) semolina
1 teaspoon baking powder
¼ cup (60ml) milk

spiced syrup
1 cup (220g) caster (superfine) sugar
1 cup (250ml) water
8 cardamom pods, bruised
2 cinnamon sticks

honey orange cream
¾ cup (180ml) thickened (heavy) cream
1 tablespoon honey
2 tablespoons finely grated orange rind

1 Preheat oven to 180°C/350°F. Grease deep 20cm (8-inch) round cake pan; line base and side with baking paper.
2 Beat butter, sugar, honey and spices in small bowl with electric mixer until light and fluffy. Beat in eggs, one at a time, until just combined between additions; transfer mixture to medium bowl. Fold in ground almonds, semolina, baking powder and milk. Spread mixture into pan.
3 Bake cake about 40 minutes. Stand cake 5 minutes.
4 Meanwhile, make spiced syrup.
5 Pour strained hot syrup over hot cake in pan; cool cake in pan to room temperature. Turn cake, in pan, upside-down onto serving plate; refrigerate 3 hours or overnight.
6 Remove cake from refrigerator. Make honey orange cream.
7 Remove cake from pan; serve cake at room temperature with honey orange cream.

spiced syrup Stir ingredients in small saucepan over heat, without boiling, until sugar dissolves; bring to the boil. Boil, uncovered, without stirring, about 5 minutes or until syrup thickens slightly.
honey orange cream Beat cream, honey and rind in small bowl with electric mixer until soft peaks form.

prep + cook time
1 hour (+ cooling, refrigeration & standing) serves 10

whipped cream cake with caramel icing

In this recipe, cream replaces milk and butter, resulting in a cake that's firm like a buttercake – even though it's made like a sponge. It is fine to use two 300ml (or one 600ml) cartons of cream for this recipe.

2⅔ cups (580ml) thickened (heavy) cream
3 eggs
1 teaspoon vanilla extract
1¼ cups (275g) firmly packed light brown sugar
2 cups (300g) self-raising flour

caramel icing
60g (2 ounces) butter
½ cup (110g) firmly packed light brown sugar
2 tablespoons milk
½ cup (80g) icing (confectioners') sugar

1 Preheat oven to 180°C/350°F. Grease deep 22cm (9-inch) round cake pan; line base with baking paper.
2 Beat half the cream in small bowl with electric mixer until soft peaks form.
3 Beat eggs and extract in small bowl with electric mixer until thick and creamy; gradually add sugar, beating until dissolved between additions. Transfer mixture to large bowl. Fold in a quarter of the whipped cream then sifted flour, then remaining whipped cream. Spread mixture into pan.
4 Bake cake about 50 minutes. Stand cake in pan 5 minutes; turn, top-side up, onto wire rack to cool.
5 Meanwhile, beat remaining cream in small bowl with electric mixer until firm peaks form.
6 Make caramel icing.
7 Split cold cake in half; sandwich layers with cream. Spread cake with caramel icing.
caramel icing Melt butter in small saucepan, add brown sugar and milk; bring to the boil. Reduce heat immediately; simmer 2 minutes. Cool to room temperature. Stir in icing sugar until smooth.

prep + cook time
1 hour 10 minutes
serves 10

big cakes

quince and blackberry crumble cake

185g (6 ounces) unsalted butter, softened
¾ cup (165g) caster (superfine) sugar
2 eggs
2¼ cups (335g) self-raising flour
¾ cup (180ml) milk
2 cups (300g) frozen blackberries
2 teaspoons cornflour (cornstarch)

poached quince
3 cups (750ml) water
¾ cup (165g) caster (superfine) sugar
1 cinnamon stick
1 tablespoon lemon juice
3 medium quinces (1kg), each cut into 8 wedges

cinnamon crumble
¾ cup (110g) plain (all-purpose) flour
2 tablespoons caster (superfine) sugar
½ cup (110g) firmly packed light brown sugar
100g (3 ounces) cold unsalted butter, chopped
1 teaspoon ground cinnamon

1 Make poached quince.
2 Preheat oven to 180°C/350°F. Grease deep 22cm (9-inch) square cake pan; line base and sides with baking paper.
3 Beat butter and sugar in small bowl with electric mixer until light and fluffy. Add eggs, one at a time, beating between additions until just combined; transfer to large bowl. Stir in sifted flour and milk, in two batches. Spread mixture into pan.
4 Bake cake 25 minutes.
5 Meanwhile, make cinnamon crumble.
6 Remove cake from oven. Working quickly, toss frozen blackberries in cornflour to coat. Top cake with drained quince then blackberries; sprinkle crumble over fruit. Return to oven; bake 20 minutes.
7 Stand cake in pan 5 minutes; turn, top-side up, onto wire rack. Serve cake warm or cold with reserved quince syrup.

poached quince Stir the water, sugar, cinnamon stick and juice in medium saucepan over low heat until sugar dissolves. Add quince; bring to the boil. Reduce heat; simmer, covered, about 1½ hours or until quince is tender and rosy in colour. Cool quince in syrup to room temperature; strain quince over medium bowl. Reserve quince and syrup separately.
cinnamon crumble Blend or process ingredients, pulsing until ingredients just come together.

prep + cook time
2 hours 45 minutes (+ cooling)
serves 16

Biscuits

Biscuits are an essential and very popular part of an afternoon tea. And their great advantage is that most of them can be made in advance (fill or ice them on the day of the tea party) which leaves you time to spend on the cake and sandwiches. Once biscuits are iced or filled they go soft very quickly.

greek almond crescents

Crescents will keep in an airtight container for up to a week.

250g (8 ounces) butter, softened
1 teaspoon vanilla extract
1 cup (220g) caster (superfine) sugar
1 egg
¼ cup (60ml) brandy
¾ cup (120g) roasted blanched almonds, chopped finely
2½ cups (375g) plain (all-purpose) flour
1½ cups (225g) self-raising flour
½ teaspoon ground nutmeg
¼ cup (60ml) rosewater
½ cup (125ml) water
3 cups (480g) icing (confectioners') sugar

1 Preheat oven to 180°C/350°F. Grease oven trays.
2 Beat butter, extract and caster sugar in small bowl with electric mixer until light and fluffy. Beat in egg and brandy; transfer mixture to large bowl. Stir in nuts and sifted flours and nutmeg, in two batches.
3 Turn dough onto floured surface; knead lightly until smooth. Shape tablespoons of dough into crescent shapes; place about 2.5cm (1 inch) apart on trays.
4 Bake about 15 minutes or until browned lightly. Lift hot crescents onto wire racks; brush with combined rosewater and the water. Coat thickly with sifted icing sugar; cool.

prep + cook time 50 minutes
makes 50

chocolate chip cookies

Dark chocolate can be replaced with milk or white chocolate. For choc-nut cookies, replace a third of the chocolate with roasted chopped nuts such as hazelnuts, walnuts, pecans or macadamias. Cookies will keep in an airtight container for up to a week.

250g (8 ounces) butter, softened
1 teaspoon vanilla extract
¾ cup (165g) caster (superfine) sugar
¾ cup (165g) firmly packed light brown sugar
1 egg
2¼ cups (335g) plain (all-purpose) flour
1 teaspoon bicarbonate of soda (baking soda)
375g (12 ounces) dark chocolate melts, chopped coarsely

1 Preheat oven to 180°C/350°F. Grease oven trays.
2 Beat butter, extract, sugars and egg in small bowl with electric mixer until light and fluffy. Transfer mixture to large bowl; stir in sifted flour and soda, in two batches. Stir in chocolate.
3 Roll tablespoons of mixture into balls; place about 5cm (2 inches) apart on trays.
4 Bake cookies about 15 minutes; cool on trays.

prep + cook time 30 minutes
makes 36

biscuits

chocolate chunk and raspberry cookies

Mix and match different coloured chocolates with different berries if you like. Store cookies in an airtight container in the fridge for up to a week.

125g (4 ounces) butter, softened
¾ cup (165g) firmly packed light brown sugar
1 egg
1 teaspoon vanilla extract
1 cup (150g) plain (all-purpose) flour
¼ cup (35g) self-raising flour
⅓ cup (35g) cocoa powder
½ teaspoon bicarbonate of soda (baking soda)
90g (3 ounces) dark eating (semi-sweet) chocolate, chopped coarsely
125g (4 ounces) frozen raspberries

1 Preheat oven to 180°C/350°F. Line oven trays with baking paper.
2 Beat butter, sugar, egg and extract in small bowl with electric mixer until combined. Stir in sifted flours, cocoa and soda, in two batches, then stir in chocolate and raspberries.
3 Drop tablespoons of mixture about 5cm (2 inches) apart onto trays; flatten slightly.
4 Bake cookies about 12 minutes. Stand cookies on trays 5 minutes before transferring to a wire rack to cool.

prep + cook time 35 minutes
makes 24

jam drops

Jam drops will keep in an airtight container for up to two days.

125g (4 ounces) butter, softened
½ teaspoon vanilla extract
½ cup (110g) caster (superfine) sugar
1 cup (120g) ground almonds
1 egg
1 cup (150g) plain (all-purpose) flour
1 teaspoon finely grated lemon rind
⅓ cup (110g) raspberry jam
2 tablespoons apricot jam

1 Preheat oven to 180°C/350°F. Line oven trays with baking paper.
2 Beat butter, extract, sugar and ground almonds in small bowl with electric mixer until light and fluffy. Beat in egg; stir in sifted flour.
3 Divide rind between both jams; mix well.
4 Roll tablespoons of mixture into balls; place about 5cm (2 inches) apart on trays, flatten slightly. Using end of a wooden spoon, press a flower shape, about 1cm (½ inch) deep, into dough; fill each hole with a little jam, using raspberry jam for petals of flowers and apricot jam for centres.
5 Bake drops about 15 minutes. Cool on trays.

prep + cook time 40 minutes
makes 24

mocha vanilla twists

Store twists in an airtight container for up to a week.

125g (4 ounces) butter, softened
½ cup (110g) caster (superfine) sugar
1 egg
1 teaspoon vanilla extract
1⅔ cups (250g) plain (all-purpose) flour
2 teaspoons instant coffee granules
2 teaspoons boiling water
2 tablespoons cocoa powder

1 Preheat oven to 180°C/350°F. Line oven trays with baking paper.
2 Beat butter, sugar, egg and extract in small bowl with electric mixer until combined; stir in sifted flour, in two batches.
3 Divide dough in half. Stir combined coffee and the water and sifted cocoa into one portion to make mocha dough.
4 Divide both dough halves into four equal portions. Roll each portion into a 40cm (16-inch) sausage. Twist one plain sausage and one mocha sausage together; cut into seven 5cm (2-inch) lengths. Repeat with remaining plain and mocha dough sausages.
5 Place twists about 2.5cm (1 inch) apart on trays.
6 Bake twists about 15 minutes. Cool on trays.

prep + cook time 45 minutes
makes 28

refrigerator slice-and-bake cookies

These basic cookies can be topped with nuts before baking or, once cooked, iced then dipped into various sprinkles, or simply dusted lightly with sifted icing sugar. If you want to flavour the dough, beat any essence or extract of your choice with the butter and sugar mixture, or beat in a teaspoon or two of finely grated citrus rind. The cookies will keep in an airtight container for at least a week.

250g (8 ounces) butter, softened
1 cup (160g) icing (confectioners') sugar
2½ cups (375g) plain (all-purpose) flour

1 Beat butter and sifted icing sugar in small bowl with electric mixer until light and fluffy. Transfer to large bowl; stir in sifted flour, in two batches.
2 Knead dough lightly on floured surface until smooth. Divide dough in half; roll each half into a 25cm (10-inch) log. Wrap logs in plastic; refrigerate about 1 hour or until firm.
3 Preheat oven to 180°C/350°F. Grease oven trays.
4 Cut logs into 1cm (½-inch) slices; place 2.5cm (1 inch) apart on trays.
5 Bake cookies about 10 minutes. Cool on trays.

prep + cook time
30 minutes (+ refrigeration)
makes 50

biscuits

amaretti

These biscuits are best if the mixture stands overnight: they will work if they're baked straight away, but they're just not quite as good. Amaretti will keep in an airtight container for at least a week.

2 egg whites
1 cup (120g) ground almonds
1 cup (220g) caster (superfine) sugar
¼ teaspoon almond extract
20 blanched almonds (20g)

1 Grease oven trays.
2 Beat egg whites, ground almonds, sugar and extract in small bowl with electric mixer for 3 minutes; stand 5 minutes.
3 Spoon mixture into piping bag fitted with 1cm (½ inch) plain tube. Pipe mixture onto trays in circular motion, from centre out, until about 4cm (1½ inches) in diameter. Top each amaretti with a nut, cover unbaked amaretti loosely with foil; stand at room temperature overnight (see note).
4 Preheat oven to 180°C/350°F.
5 Bake amaretti about 12 minutes. Stand on trays 5 minutes before transferring to a wire rack to cool.

prep + cook time
30 minutes (+ standing)
makes 20

malted milk flowers

Store biscuits in an airtight container for up to a week.

125g (4 ounces) butter, softened
½ cup (110g) caster (superfine) sugar
1 egg
2 tablespoons golden syrup or treacle
⅓ cup (40g) malted milk powder
2½ cups (375g) plain (all-purpose) flour
½ teaspoon bicarbonate of soda (baking soda)
1½ teaspoons cream of tartar
18 chocolate freckles
18 dark chocolate melts

malt icing
1½ cups (240g) icing (confectioners') sugar
2 tablespoons malted milk powder
2 tablespoons milk, approximately

1 Beat butter, sugar and egg in small bowl with electric mixer until combined. Transfer mixture to large bowl; stir in golden syrup and sifted dry ingredients, in two batches.
2 Knead dough lightly on floured surface until smooth. Cover; refrigerate 30 minutes.
3 Preheat oven to 150°C/300°F. Line oven trays with baking paper.
4 Roll dough between sheets of baking paper until 5mm (¼-inch) thick. Cut 7.5cm (3-inch) flowers from dough; place flowers about 2.5cm (1 inch) apart on trays.
5 Bake biscuits about 18 minutes. Cool on trays.
6 Meanwhile, make malt icing.
7 Spread biscuits with icing; top half the biscuits with freckles and remaining biscuits with chocolate melts.

malt icing Sift icing sugar and malted milk powder into small heatproof bowl; stir in enough milk to make a thick paste. Stir over small saucepan of simmering water until icing is spreadable.

prep + cook time
50 minutes (+ refrigeration)
makes 36

biscuits

chocolate wheaties

If the weather is cool, store biscuits in an airtight container at room temperature – refrigerate them if the weather is hot.

90g (3 ounces) butter, softened
½ cup (110g) firmly packed light brown sugar
1 egg
¼ cup (20g) desiccated coconut
⅓ cup (35g) wheat germ
⅔ cup (100g) wholemeal plain (all-purpose) flour
⅓ cup (50g) white self-raising flour
185g (6 ounces) dark eating (semi-sweet) chocolate, melted

1 Beat butter and sugar in small bowl with electric mixer until smooth. Beat in egg until combined. Stir in coconut, wheat germ and sifted flours.
2 Roll dough between sheets of baking paper until 5mm (¼-inch) thick. Place on tray; refrigerate 30 minutes.
3 Preheat oven to 180°C/350°F. Line oven trays with baking paper.
4 Cut 7.5cm (3-inch) rounds from dough; place rounds about 2.5cm (1 inch) apart on trays.
5 Bake wheaties about 20 minutes. Cool on trays.
6 Spread bases of wheaties with chocolate; mark with a fork. Stand at room temperature until set.

prep + cook time 50 minutes (+ refrigeration & standing)
makes 18

traditional shortbread

Ground white rice can be used instead of rice flour, although it is slightly coarser in texture. Store shortbread in an airtight container for up to a week.

250g (8 ounces) butter, softened
⅓ cup (75g) caster (superfine) sugar
1 tablespoon water
2 cups (300g) plain (all-purpose) flour
½ cup (90g) rice flour
2 tablespoons white (granulated) sugar

1 Preheat oven to 160°C/325°F. Grease oven trays.
2 Beat butter and caster sugar in medium bowl with electric mixer until light and fluffy; stir in the water and sifted flours, in two batches. Knead mixture on floured surface until smooth.
3 Divide mixture in half; shape each half on separate trays into 20cm (8-inch) rounds. Mark each round into 12 wedges; prick with fork. Pinch edges of rounds with fingers; sprinkle shortbread with white sugar.
4 Bake shortbread about 40 minutes. Stand on trays 5 minutes. Using sharp knife, cut into wedges along marked lines. Cool on trays.

prep + cook time 1 hour
makes 24

biscuits

melting moments

Unfilled biscuits will keep in an airtight container for up to a week. Filled biscuits will keep for a few days in an airtight container in the fridge.

250g (8 ounces) butter, softened
1 teaspoon vanilla extract
½ cup (80g) icing (confectioners') sugar
1½ cups (225g) plain (all-purpose) flour
½ cup (75g) cornflour (cornstarch)

butter cream
90g (3 ounces) butter
¾ cup (120g) icing (confectioners') sugar
1 teaspoon finely grated lemon rind
1 teaspoon lemon juice

1 Preheat oven to 160°C/325°F. Line oven trays with baking paper.
2 Beat butter, extract and sifted icing sugar in small bowl with electric mixer until light and fluffy. Transfer mixture to large bowl; stir in sifted flours, in two batches.
3 With floured hands, roll rounded teaspoons of mixture into balls; place about 2.5cm (1 inch) apart on trays. Flatten slightly with a floured fork.
4 Bake biscuits about 15 minutes. Stand on trays 5 minutes before transferring to a wire rack to cool.
5 Make butter cream.
6 Sandwich biscuits with butter cream. Dust with extra sifted icing sugar before serving, if you like.

butter cream Beat butter, sifted icing sugar and rind in small bowl with electric mixer until pale and fluffy; beat in juice.

prep + cook time 40 minutes
makes 25

baklava twists

250g (8 ounces) butter, softened
¼ cup (55g) caster (superfine) sugar
1 vanilla extract
1½ cups (185g) plain (all-purpose) flour
2 teaspoons rosewater

nut topping
⅔ cup (90g) roasted unsalted shelled pistachios, chopped finely
2 tablespoons honey
3 teaspoons rosewater

1 Make nut topping.
2 Preheat oven to 180°C/350°F. Line oven trays with baking paper.
3 Beat butter, sugar and extract in small bowl with electric mixer until smooth. Transfer mixture to large bowl; stir in sifted flour, in two batches. Stir in rosewater.
4 Roll rounded teaspoons of mixture into balls; roll each ball into 12cm (4½-inch) log. Twist each log into a loop, overlapping one end over the other. Place twists about 2.5cm (1 inch) apart on trays. Top each twist with about ½ teaspoon nut topping.
5 Bake twists about 10 minutes. Cool on trays.

nut topping Combine ingredients in small bowl.

prep + cook time 45 minutes
makes 42

biscuits

chocolate caramel shortbread cookies

You will need three 120g (4-ounce) packets round shortbread biscuits for this recipe. The biscuits should be 6cm (2¼ inches) in diameter. Store filled and chocolate-dipped cookies in an airtight container in the fridge for up to a week.

18 round shortbread biscuits (360g) (see notes)
185g (6 ounces) dark eating (semi-sweet) chocolate, chopped coarsely
2 teaspoons vegetable oil
caramel filling
½ cup (110g) firmly packed light brown sugar
60g (2 ounces) butter, chopped
2 teaspoons water
1½ tablespoons cornflour (cornstarch)
½ cup (125ml) milk
1 egg yolk
1 teaspoon vanilla extract

1 Make caramel filling.
2 Spread caramel filling over half the shortbread biscuits; top with remaining biscuits. Cover; refrigerate 1 hour.
3 Melt chocolate in small heatproof bowl over saucepan of simmering water (do not allow water to touch base of bowl). Remove from heat; stir in oil.
4 Dip one side of cookies in melted chocolate. Stand at room temperature until set.
caramel filling Stir sugar, butter and the water in small saucepan over heat until sugar is dissolved. Stir in blended cornflour and milk; stir over heat until mixture boils and thickens. Remove from heat; whisk in egg yolk and extract. Cover surface of caramel with plastic wrap; refrigerate 3 hours or overnight.

prep + cook time
25 minutes (+ refrigeration)
makes 9

brandy snaps

Bake the first tray of snaps and while they are cooking prepare the next tray of snaps; put them into the oven as you're getting the first batch out. If you handle four snaps at a time, the process will be easy. Snaps are best made on the day of serving. It is fine to use just one 300ml carton of cream for this recipe.

90g (3 ounces) butter
½ cup (110g) firmly packed dark brown sugar
⅓ cup (115g) golden syrup or treacle
1 teaspoon ground ginger
⅔ cup (100g) plain (all-purpose) flour
1 teaspoon lemon juice
1¼ cups (310ml) thickened (heavy) cream, whipped

1 Preheat oven to 180°C/350°F. Grease oven trays.
2 Stir butter, sugar, syrup and ginger in medium saucepan, over low heat, until smooth. Remove from heat; stir in sifted flour and juice.
3 Drop rounded teaspoons of mixture about 5cm (2 inches) apart onto trays. Using a wet, thin metal spatula, spread mixture into 8cm (3¼-inch) rounds.
4 Bake snaps about 8 minutes or until bubbling and golden brown. Working quickly, slide a thin metal spatula under each snap; shape each one into a cone. Place on wire rack to cool. Fill with whipped cream just before serving.

prep + cook time 40 minutes
makes 32

biscuits

spicy fruit mince pillows

Pillows will keep in an airtight container at room temperature for up to a week.

90g (3 ounces) butter, softened
⅓ cup (55g) icing (confectioners') sugar
1 egg
1¼ cups (185g) plain (all-purpose) flour
¼ cup (35g) self-raising flour
2 tablespoons milk
2 teaspoons caster (superfine) sugar

spicy fruit filling
2⅔ cups (375g) seeded dried dates, chopped coarsely
¾ cup (180ml) water
2 teaspoons ground allspice
¼ teaspoon ground cloves
pinch bicarbonate of soda (baking soda)

1 Beat butter and sifted icing sugar in small bowl with electric mixer until smooth. Beat in egg until combined. Stir in sifted flours, in two batches. Cover dough; refrigerate 30 minutes.
2 Meanwhile, make spicy fruit filling.
3 Preheat oven to 180°C/350°F. Line oven trays with baking paper.
4 Roll dough between sheets of baking paper to 30cm x 40cm (12-inch x 16-inch) rectangle; cut into four 7.5cm x 40cm (3-inch x 16-inch) strips.
5 Spoon filling into piping bag fitted with large 1.5cm (¾-inch) plain tube; pipe filling down centre of each strip. Fold edges in until they meet to enclose filling; turn seam-side down onto board. Cut each roll into 10 pillow shapes; place pillows, seam-side down, on trays; brush with milk, sprinkle with caster sugar.
6 Bake pillows about 20 minutes. Cool on trays.

spicy fruit filling Place dates and the water in medium saucepan; cook, stirring, about 10 minutes or until thick and smooth. Stir in spices and soda. Cool.

prep + cook time
50 minutes (+ refrigeration)
makes 40

lime and ginger kisses

Unfilled biscuits will keep in an airtight container for up to a week. Filled biscuits will keep for a few days in an airtight container in the fridge.

125g (4 ounces) butter, softened
½ cup (110g) firmly packed light brown sugar
1 egg
¼ cup (35g) plain (all-purpose) flour
¼ cup (35g) self-raising flour
¾ cup (110g) cornflour (cornstarch)
2 teaspoons ground ginger
½ teaspoon ground cinnamon
¼ teaspoon ground cloves
lime butter cream
60g (2 ounces) butter, softened
2 teaspoons finely grated lime rind
¾ cup (120g) icing (confectioners') sugar
2 teaspoons milk

1 Preheat oven to 180°C/350°F. Line oven trays with baking paper.
2 Beat butter, sugar and egg in small bowl with electric mixer until smooth. Stir in sifted dry ingredients.
3 Roll heaped teaspoons of mixture into balls; place balls about 5cm (2 inches) apart on trays.
4 Bake biscuits about 10 minutes. Loosen biscuits; cool on trays.
5 Meanwhile, make lime butter cream.
6 Sandwich biscuits with butter cream.

lime butter cream Beat butter and rind in small bowl with electric mixer until as white as possible. Beat in sifted icing sugar and milk, in two batches.

prep + cook time
35 minutes (+ cooling)
makes 18

hazelnut moments with choc berry filling

Unfilled biscuits will keep in an airtight container for up to a week. Filled biscuits will keep for a few days in an airtight container in the fridge.

90g (3 ounces) butter, softened
½ teaspoon vanilla extract
¼ cup (55g) caster (superfine) sugar
1 egg
½ cup (50g) ground hazelnuts
¾ cup (110g) plain (all-purpose) flour
¼ cup (25g) cocoa powder

choc berry filling
90g (3 ounces) dark eating (semi-sweet) chocolate, melted
60g (2 ounces) butter, softened
⅓ cup (110g) chocolate hazelnut spread
¼ cup (35g) fresh raspberries, chopped coarsely

1 Beat butter, extract, sugar and egg in small bowl with electric mixer until combined. Stir in ground hazelnuts, then sifted flour and cocoa.
2 Divide dough in half; roll each half between sheets of baking paper until 3mm (⅛-inch) thick. Refrigerate 30 minutes.
3 Preheat oven to 180°C/350°F. Line oven trays with baking paper.
4 Cut dough into 4cm (1½-inch) fluted rounds; place on trays 2.5cm (1 inch) apart.
5 Bake biscuits about 8 minutes. Cool on trays.
6 Make choc berry filling.
7 Spoon choc berry filling into piping bag fitted with 2cm (¾-inch) fluted tube. Pipe filling onto flat side of half the biscuits; top with remaining biscuits.

choc berry filling Beat cooled chocolate, butter and spread in small bowl with electric mixer until thick and glossy. Fold in raspberries.

prep + cook time 30 minutes (+ refrigeration & cooling)
makes 24

coconut chocolate crunchies

Unfilled biscuits will keep in an airtight container for up to a week. Filled biscuits will keep for a few days in an airtight container in the fridge.

125g (4 ounces) butter, softened
¾ cup (165g) firmly packed light brown sugar
1 tablespoon golden syrup or treacle
2 eggs
2 cups (300g) self-raising flour
1 cup (80g) desiccated coconut
½ cup (45g) quick-cooking oats
milk chocolate ganache
185g (6 ounces) milk eating chocolate, chopped coarsely
30g (1 ounce) butter

1 Preheat oven to 180°C/350°F. Line oven trays with baking paper.
2 Beat butter, sugar and syrup in small bowl with electric mixer until smooth. Beat in eggs, one at a time. Stir in sifted flour, coconut and oats.
3 Roll rounded teaspoons of mixture into balls; place about 5cm (2 inches) apart on trays. Flatten with fork.
4 Bake biscuits about 12 minutes. Cool on trays.
5 Meanwhile, make milk chocolate ganache.
6 Sandwich biscuits with ganache; refrigerate until firm.
milk chocolate ganache Stir chocolate and butter in small heatproof bowl over small saucepan of simmering water until smooth; cool.

prep + cook time 40 minutes
(+ refrigeration & cooling)
makes 40

wagonettes

You need two 200g (6½-ounce) packets milk chocolate wheaten biscuits for this recipe. If the marshmallow sets too quickly, return it to the mixer bowl with about 1 tablespoon boiling water and beat it for about a minute. Unfilled biscuits will keep in an airtight container for up to a week. Filled biscuits will keep for a few days in an airtight container in the fridge.

⅓ cup (75g) caster (superfine) sugar
⅓ cup (80ml) water
2 teaspoons gelatine
⅓ cup (110g) strawberry jam, warmed, strained
32 (400g) milk chocolate wheaten biscuits (see notes)
½ teaspoon vanilla extract
pink food colouring

1 Stir sugar and half the water in small saucepan over low heat until sugar dissolves.
2 Combine gelatine and the remaining water in small jug. Pour gelatine mixture into hot sugar syrup; stir over medium heat about 3 minutes or until gelatine dissolves. Pour mixture into small heatproof bowl; cool.
3 Spread jam onto the plain side of half the biscuits.
4 To make marshmallow, beat gelatine mixture in small bowl with electric mixer on high speed about 8 minutes or until very thick. Beat in extract and a few drops of food colouring.
5 Spoon marshmallow into piping bag fitted with 2cm (¾-inch) plain tube. Pipe marshmallow over jam; top with remaining biscuits.

prep + cook time
30 minutes (+ cooling)
makes 16

passionfruit meringue kisses

2 egg whites
½ cup (110g) caster (superfine) sugar
yellow food colouring
1 teaspoon strained passionfruit juice
1 teaspoon cornflour (cornstarch)
passionfruit butter
60g (2 ounces) unsalted butter, softened
¾ cup (120g) icing (confectioners') sugar
1 tablespoon passionfruit pulp

1 Preheat oven to 120°C/250°F. Grease oven trays; line with baking paper.
2 Beat egg whites, sugar and a few drops of food colouring in small bowl with electric mixer about 15 minutes or until sugar dissolves. Fold in juice and cornflour.
3 Spoon meringue mixture into piping bag fitted with 2cm (¾-inch) fluted tube; pipe 4cm (1½-inch) stars onto trays 2cm (¾ inch) apart.
4 Bake meringues about 1 hour. Cool on trays.
5 Meanwhile, make passionfruit butter.
6 Sandwich meringues with passionfruit butter.
passionfruit butter Beat butter and sifted icing sugar in small bowl with electric mixer until light and fluffy. Stir in pulp.

prep + cook time
1 hour 25 minutes (+ cooling)
makes 24

biscuits

pistachio, white chocolate and honey french macaroons

⅓ cup (45g) roasted unsalted shelled pistachios
3 egg whites
¼ cup (55g) caster (superfine) sugar
green food colouring
1¼ cups (200g) icing (confectioners') sugar
¾ cup (90g) ground almonds

honeyed white chocolate ganache
¼ cup (60ml) pouring cream
155g (5 ounces) white eating chocolate, chopped coarsely
2 teaspoons honey

1 Preheat oven to 150°C/300°F. Grease oven trays; line with baking paper.
2 Process nuts until finely ground.
3 Beat egg whites in small bowl with electric mixer until soft peaks form. Add caster sugar and few drops food colouring, beat until sugar dissolves. Transfer mixture to large bowl; fold in ¼ cup of the ground pistachios, sifted icing sugar and ground almonds, in two batches.
4 Spoon mixture into piping bag fitted with 1cm (½-inch) plain tube. Pipe 4cm (1½-inch) rounds about 2.5cm (1 inch) apart onto trays. Tap trays on bench so macaroons spread slightly. Sprinkle macaroons with remaining ground pistachios; stand 30 minutes.
5 Bake macaroons about 20 minutes. Cool on trays.
6 Meanwhile, make honeyed white chocolate ganache.
7 Sandwich macaroons with ganache.

honeyed white chocolate ganache Bring cream to the boil in small saucepan. Remove from heat; pour over chocolate and honey in small bowl, stir until smooth. Stand at room temperature until spreadable.

prep + cook time
45 minutes (+ standing)
makes 16

chocolate french macaroons

Buttered brazil nuts are toffee-coated nuts; they're available from nut shops and gourmet food stores.

3 egg whites
¼ cup (55g) caster (superfine) sugar
1¼ cups (200g) icing (confectioners') sugar
¾ cup (90g) ground almonds
¼ cup (25g) cocoa powder
dark chocolate ganache
¼ cup (60ml) pouring cream
155g (5 ounces) dark eating (semi-sweet) chocolate, chopped coarsely
1 tablespoon finely crushed buttered brazil nuts

1 Preheat oven to 150°C/300°F. Grease oven trays; line with baking paper.
2 Beat egg whites in small bowl with electric mixer until soft peaks form. Add caster sugar; beat until sugar dissolves. Transfer mixture to large bowl. Fold in sifted icing sugar, ground almonds and sifted cocoa, in two batches.
3 Spoon mixture into piping bag fitted with 1cm (½-inch) plain tube. Pipe 4cm (1½-inch) rounds about 2.5cm (1 inch) apart onto trays. Tap trays on bench so macaroons spread slightly. Stand 30 minutes.
4 Bake macaroons about 20 minutes. Cool on trays.
5 Meanwhile, make dark chocolate ganache.
6 Sandwich macaroons with ganache.
dark chocolate ganache
Bring cream to the boil in small saucepan. Remove from heat; pour over chocolate in small bowl, stir until smooth. Stir in nuts. Stand at room temperature until spreadable.

prep + cook time
45 minutes (+ standing)
makes 16

coconut french macaroons

3 egg whites
¼ cup (55g) caster (superfine) sugar
½ teaspoon coconut essence
1¼ cups (200g) icing (confectioners') sugar
¾ cup (90g) ground almonds
¼ cup (20g) desiccated coconut
1 tablespoon icing (confectioners') sugar, extra

white chocolate ganache
¼ cup (60ml) pouring cream
155g (5 ounces) white eating chocolate, chopped coarsely
2 teaspoons coconut-flavoured liqueur

1 Preheat oven to 150°C/300°F. Grease oven trays; line with baking paper.
2 Beat egg whites in small bowl with electric mixer until soft peaks form. Add caster sugar and essence, beat until sugar dissolves; transfer mixture to large bowl. Fold in sifted icing sugar, ground almonds and coconut, in two batches.
3 Spoon mixture into piping bag fitted with 1cm (½-inch) plain tube. Pipe 4cm (1½-inch) rounds about 2.5cm (1 inch) apart onto trays. Tap trays on bench so macaroons spread slightly. Stand 30 minutes.
4 Bake macaroons about 20 minutes. Cool on trays.
5 Meanwhile, make white chocolate ganache.
6 Sandwich macaroons with ganache. Serve dusted with extra sifted icing sugar.

white chocolate ganache
Bring cream to the boil in small saucepan. Remove from heat; pour over chocolate in small bowl, stir until smooth. Stir in liqueur. Stand at room temperature until spreadable.

prep + cook time
45 minutes (+ standing)
makes 16

strawberry french macaroons

3 egg whites
¼ cup (55g) caster (superfine) sugar
pink food colouring
2 large (70g) fresh or frozen strawberries
1¼ cups (200g) icing (confectioners') sugar
1 cup (120g) ground almonds
⅓ cup (110g) strawberry jam
1 tablespoon icing (confectioners') sugar, extra

1 Preheat oven to 150°C/300°F. Grease oven trays; line with baking paper.
2 Beat egg whites in small bowl with electric mixer until soft peaks form. Add caster sugar and few drops food colouring, beat until sugar dissolves. Transfer mixture to large bowl.
3 Meanwhile, push fresh strawberries (or thawed frozen berries) through a fine sieve; you need 1 tablespoon of strawberry puree.
4 Fold sifted icing sugar, ground almonds and strawberry puree into egg white mixture, in two batches.
5 Spoon mixture into piping bag fitted with 1cm (½-inch) plain tube. Pipe 4cm (1½-inch) rounds about 2.5cm (1 inch) apart onto trays. Tap trays on bench so macaroons spread slightly. Stand 30 minutes.
6 Bake macaroons about 20 minutes. Cool on trays.
7 Sandwich macaroons with jam. Dust with extra sifted icing sugar.

prep + cook time
40 minutes (+ standing)
makes 16

monte carlos

185g (6 ounces) unsalted butter, softened
1 teaspoon vanilla extract
½ cup (110g) firmly packed light brown sugar
1 egg
1¼ cups (185g) self-raising flour
¾ cup (110g) plain (all-purpose) flour
½ cup (40g) desiccated coconut
½ cup (160g) raspberry jam
cream filling
60g (2 ounces) unsalted butter, softened
¾ cup (120g) icing (confectioners') sugar
½ teaspoon vanilla extract
2 teaspoons milk

1 Preheat oven to 180°C/325°F. Grease oven trays.
2 Beat butter, extract and sugar in small bowl with electric mixer until light and fluffy. Add egg, beat until combined. Stir in sifted flours and coconut.
3 Shape level teaspoons of dough into oval shapes; place about 4cm (1½ inches) apart on trays. Rough surface with fork.
4 Bake biscuits about 12 minutes. Cool on trays.
5 Meanwhile, make cream filling.
6 Place ½ teaspoon each of jam and cream filling in centre of half the biscuits; top with remaining biscuits, gently press together.
cream filling Beat butter and sifted icing sugar in small bowl with electric mixer until light and fluffy. Beat in extract and milk.

prep + cook time 50 minutes
makes 50

passionfruit cream biscuits

You need about six passionfruit for this recipe.

125g (4 ounces) butter, softened
2 teaspoons finely grated lemon rind
⅓ cup (75g) caster (superfine) sugar
2 tablespoons golden syrup or treacle
1 cup (150g) self-raising flour
⅔ cup (100g) plain (all-purpose) flour
¼ cup (60ml) passionfruit pulp
passionfruit cream
2 tablespoons passionfruit pulp
90g (3 ounces) butter, softened
1 cup (160g) icing (confectioners') sugar

1 Beat butter, rind and sugar in small bowl with electric mixer until light and fluffy. Add golden syrup, beat until combined. Stir in sifted flours and pulp.
2 Turn dough onto floured surface, knead gently until smooth. Cut dough in half; roll each portion between sheets of baking paper to 5mm (¼-inch) thickness. Refrigerate 30 minutes.
3 Preheat oven to 180°C/350°F. Grease oven trays; line with baking paper.
4 Cut 25 x 4cm (1½-inch) fluted rounds from each portion of dough; place about 2.5cm (1 inch) apart on trays.
5 Bake biscuits about 10 minutes. Cool on trays.

6 Meanwhile, make passionfruit cream.
7 Spoon passionfruit cream into piping bag fitted with 5mm (¼-inch) fluted tube. Pipe cream onto half the biscuits; top with remaining biscuits. Serve dusted with a little extra sifted icing sugar, if you like.
passionfruit cream Strain passionfruit pulp through fine sieve into small jug, discard seeds. Beat butter and sugar in small bowl with electric mixer until light and fluffy. Beat in passionfruit juice.

prep + cook time 45 minutes (+ refrigeration & cooling)
makes 25

hazelnut pinwheels

Store pinwheels in an airtight container for up to a week.

1¼ cups (185g) plain (all-purpose) flour
100g (3 ounces) cold butter, chopped
½ cup (110g) caster (superfine) sugar
1 egg yolk
1 tablespoon milk, approximately
⅓ cup (110g) chocolate hazelnut spread
2 tablespoons ground hazelnuts

1 Process flour, butter and sugar until crumbly. Add egg yolk; process with enough milk until mixture forms a ball. Knead dough on floured surface until smooth. Wrap in plastic; refrigerate 1 hour.
2 Roll dough between sheets of baking paper into a 20cm x 30cm (8-inch x 12-inch) rectangle; remove top sheet of paper. Spread dough evenly with spread; sprinkle with ground hazelnuts. Using bottom sheet of paper as a guide, roll dough tightly from one long side to enclose filling. Wrap roll in plastic; refrigerate 30 minutes.
3 Preheat oven to 180°C/350°F. Grease oven trays; line with baking paper.
4 Remove plastic from dough. Cut roll into 1cm (½-inch) slices; place on trays 2cm (¾ inch) apart.
5 Bake pinwheels about 20 minutes. Stand on trays 5 minutes before transferring to a wire rack to cool.

prep + cook time
40 minutes (+ refrigeration)
makes 30

linzer biscuits

The 2.5cm (1-inch) fluted centre rounds can be baked for about 10 minutes; sandwich with extra jam. You can substitute the fig and ginger jam for any jam of your choice. These biscuits are best served on the day they are made. Store unfilled biscuits in an airtight container for up to a week.

⅔ cup (100g) plain (all-purpose) flour
⅔ cup (150g) caster (superfine) sugar
1½ cups (180g) finely chopped walnuts
1 hard-boiled egg yolk
90g (3 ounces) butter, chopped coarsely
1 egg yolk
⅔ cup (220g) fig and ginger jam
1 tablespoon icing (confectioners') sugar

1 Combine sifted flour, caster sugar, nuts and hard-boiled egg yolk in medium bowl; rub in butter. Stir in egg yolk until ingredients come together.
2 Turn dough onto floured surface, knead gently until smooth. Divide dough in half; roll each portion between sheets of baking paper to 3mm (⅛-inch) thickness. Refrigerate 30 minutes.
3 Preheat oven to 160°C/325°F. Grease oven trays; line with baking paper.
4 Cut 24 x 5cm (2-inch) fluted rounds from each portion of dough; place about 2.5cm (1 inch) apart on trays. Cut 2.5cm (1-inch) fluted rounds from centre of half the rounds.
5 Bake biscuits about 15 minutes. Cool on trays.
6 Sandwich biscuits with jam. Serve dusted with sifted icing sugar.

prep + cook time 50 minutes (+ refrigeration & cooling)
makes 24

coffee almond biscuits

Store in an airtight container for up to a week.

1 tablespoon instant coffee granules
3 teaspoons hot water
3 cups (360g) ground almonds
1 cup (220g) caster (superfine) sugar
2 tablespoons coffee-flavoured liqueur
3 egg whites, beaten lightly
24 coffee beans

1 Preheat oven to 180°C/350°F. Grease oven trays; line with baking paper.
2 Dissolve coffee in the hot water in a large bowl. Stir in ground almonds, sugar, liqueur and egg whites until mixture forms a firm paste.
3 Roll level tablespoons of mixture into balls; place on trays 3cm (1¼ inches) apart; flatten with hand. Press coffee beans into tops of biscuits.
4 Bake biscuits about 15 minutes. Cool on trays.

prep + cook time 30 minutes
makes 24

vanilla bean thins

1 vanilla bean
30g (1 ounce) butter, softened
¼ cup (55g) caster (superfine) sugar
1 egg white, beaten lightly
¼ cup (35g) plain (all-purpose) flour

1 Preheat oven to 200°C/400°F. Grease oven trays; line with baking paper.
2 Halve vanilla bean lengthways; scrape seeds into medium bowl, discard pod. Add butter and sugar to bowl; stir until combined. Stir in egg white and sifted flour.
3 Spoon mixture into piping bag fitted with 5mm (¼-inch) plain tube. Pipe 6cm (2¼-inch) long strips (making them slightly wider at both ends) about 5cm (2 inches) apart on trays.
4 Bake biscuits about 5 minutes or until edges are browned lightly. Cool on trays.

prep + cook time 25 minutes
makes 24

chocolate lace crisps

100g (3 ounces) dark eating (semi-sweet) chocolate, chopped coarsely
80g (2½ ounces) butter, chopped
1 cup (220g) caster (superfine) sugar
1 egg, beaten lightly
1 cup (150g) plain (all-purpose) flour
2 tablespoons cocoa powder
¼ teaspoon bicarbonate of soda (baking soda)
¼ cup (40g) icing (confectioners') sugar

1 Melt chocolate and butter in small saucepan over low heat. Transfer to medium bowl.
2 Stir in caster sugar, egg and sifted flour, cocoa and soda. Cover; refrigerate 15 minutes or until mixture is firm enough to handle.
3 Preheat oven to 180°C/350°F. Grease oven trays; line with baking paper.
4 Roll level tablespoons of mixture into balls; roll each ball in icing sugar, place on trays 8cm (3¼ inches) apart.
5 Bake crisps about 15 minutes. Cool on trays.

prep + cook time
45 minutes (+ refrigeration)
makes 24

Slices

These slices are richer and more luscious than usual. They're special afternoon tea slices, filled with caramel or fruit, spread with tart lemon icing or drizzled with melted chocolate. If you are serving a lot of rich food cut these into smaller slices – just one mouthful will be enough.

chocolate caramel slice

The slice will keep in an airtight container in the refrigerator for up to 4 days.

½ cup (75g) self-raising flour
½ cup (75g) plain (all-purpose) flour
1 cup (80g) desiccated coconut
1 cup (220g) firmly packed light brown sugar
125g (4 ounces) butter, melted
395g (14 ounces) canned sweetened condensed milk
30g (1 ounce) butter, extra
2 tablespoons golden syrup or treacle
185g (6 ounces) dark eating (semi-sweet) chocolate, chopped coarsely
2 teaspoons vegetable oil

1 Preheat oven to 180°C/350°F. Grease 20cm x 30cm (8-inch x 12-inch) rectangular pan; line base and long sides with baking paper, extending paper 5cm (2 inches) over sides.
2 Combine sifted flours, coconut, sugar and butter in medium bowl; press mixture evenly over base of pan.
3 Bake about 15 minutes or until browned lightly.
4 Meanwhile, make caramel filling by combining condensed milk, extra butter and syrup in small saucepan. Stir over medium heat about 15 minutes or until caramel mixture is golden brown; pour over base. Bake 10 minutes; cool.

5 Make topping by combining chocolate and oil in small saucepan; stir over low heat until smooth. Pour warm topping over cold caramel. Refrigerate 3 hours or overnight.

prep + cook time 45 minutes (+ cooling & refrigeration)
makes 24

rich hazelnut slice

Slice will keep in an airtight container in the refrigerator for up to a week.

250g (8 ounces) plain chocolate biscuits
¾ cup (110g) roasted hazelnuts, chopped coarsely
155g (5 ounces) unsalted butter, melted
395g (14 ounces) canned sweetened condensed milk
375g (12 ounces) milk eating chocolate, chopped coarsely
315g (10 ounces) dark eating (semi-sweet) chocolate, chopped coarsely
15g (½ ounce) unsalted butter, extra
30g (1 ounce) white eating chocolate, melted

1 Grease 20cm x 30cm (8-inch x 12-inch) rectangular pan; line base and long sides with baking paper, extending paper 5cm (2 inches) over sides.
2 Process biscuits and ¼ cup of the nuts until fine; add butter, process until combined. Press mixture over base of pan. Refrigerate about 20 minutes or until firm.
3 Stir condensed milk and 345g (11 ounces) of the milk chocolate in small saucepan over low heat until smooth. Stir in remaining nuts. Working quickly, spread chocolate mixture over base.
4 Stir dark chocolate and extra butter in small saucepan over low heat until smooth. Spread over milk chocolate layer.
5 Melt remaining milk chocolate; drizzle milk and white chocolate over slice. Refrigerate 20 minutes or until firm.

prep + cook time
30 minutes (+ refrigeration)
makes 32

fruity choc chip slice

Slice can be stored in an airtight container for up to a week.

⅓ cup (75g) firmly packed light brown sugar
90g (3 ounces) butter, chopped coarsely
1¼ cups (185g) plain (all-purpose) flour
1 egg yolk

fruity choc chip topping
2 eggs
1 cup (220g) firmly packed light brown sugar
⅓ cup (50g) self-raising flour
1 cup (190g) milk choc bits
1 cup (90g) rolled oats
½ cup (40g) shredded coconut
⅓ cup (45g) coarsely chopped, roasted unsalted shelled pistachios
½ cup (80g) finely chopped dried mixed berries
½ cup (30g) finely chopped dried apple

1 Preheat oven to 180°C/350°F. Grease 20cm x 30cm (8-inch x 12-inch) rectangular pan; line base and long sides with baking paper, extending paper 5cm (2 inches) over sides.
2 Stir sugar and butter in medium saucepan over low heat until smooth. Remove from heat; stir in sifted flour then egg yolk. Press mixture firmly over base of pan.
3 Bake about 10 minutes or until browned lightly. Cool.
4 Meanwhile, make fruity choc chip topping.
5 Spread topping over base; bake about 25 minutes or until browned lightly. Cool in pan.

fruity choc chip topping Beat eggs and sugar in small bowl with electric mixer until thick and pale, transfer to large bowl; fold in sifted flour then remaining ingredients.

prep + cook time 1 hour
makes 24

choc nut and cornflake slice

125g (4 ounces) butter, chopped coarsely
½ cup (110g) caster (superfine) sugar
⅓ cup (80ml) light corn syrup
⅓ cup (95g) crunchy peanut butter
4 cups (160g) cornflakes
350g (11 ounces) milk eating chocolate, melted

1 Grease 20cm x 30cm (8-inch x 12-inch) rectangular pan; line base and long sides with baking paper, extending paper 5cm (2 inches) over sides.
2 Stir butter, sugar, corn syrup and peanut butter in large saucepan over low heat until sugar dissolves. Bring to the boil. Reduce heat; simmer, uncovered, without stirring, 5 minutes. Gently stir in cornflakes. Spread mixture into pan; press firmly. Refrigerate about 30 minutes or until set.
3 Spread chocolate over slice; stand at room temperature until set.

prep + cook time
30 minutes (+ refrigeration)
makes 24

slices

raspberry coconut slice

Slice can be stored in an airtight container for up to a week.

90g (3 ounces) butter, softened
½ cup (110g) caster (superfine) sugar
1 egg
¼ cup (35g) self-raising flour
⅔ cup (100g) plain (all-purpose) flour
1 tablespoon custard powder
⅔ cup (220g) raspberry jam
coconut topping
2 cups (160g) desiccated coconut
¼ cup (55g) caster (superfine) sugar
2 eggs, beaten lightly

1 Preheat oven to 180°C/350°F. Grease 20cm x 30cm (8-inch x 12-inch) rectangular pan; line base and long sides with baking paper, extending paper 5cm (2 inches) over sides.
2 Beat butter, sugar and egg in small bowl with electric mixer until light and fluffy. Transfer to medium bowl; stir in sifted flours and custard powder. Spread dough into pan; spread with jam.
3 Make coconut topping; sprinkle over jam.
4 Bake slice about 40 minutes; cool in pan.
coconut topping Combine ingredients in medium bowl.

prep + cook time 1 hour
makes 16

lattice slice with passionfruit icing

You need to buy two packets of lattice biscuits for this recipe. The slice will keep in an airtight container in the refrigerator for up to 4 days.

2 teaspoons gelatine
2 tablespoons water
250g (8 ounces) cream cheese, softened
250g (8 ounces) unsalted butter, softened
½ cup (110g) caster (superfine) sugar
1 teaspoon vanilla extract
2 tablespoons lemon juice
35 square lattice biscuits (350g) (see notes)

passionfruit icing
2 cups (320g) icing (confectioners') sugar
2 teaspoons unsalted butter
2 tablespoons passionfruit pulp
2 teaspoons hot water, approximately

1 Grease 20cm x 30cm (8-inch x 12-inch) rectangular pan; line base and long sides with baking paper, extending paper 5cm (2 inches) over sides.
2 Sprinkle gelatine over the water in small heatproof jug; stand jug in small saucepan of simmering water, stir until gelatine dissolves.
3 Beat cream cheese, butter, sugar and extract in small bowl with electric mixer until smooth. Stir in juice and gelatine mixture.
4 Line base of pan with half the biscuits; trim biscuits to fit, if necessary. Spread cream cheese filling evenly over biscuit base; top with remaining biscuits.
5 Make passionfruit icing.
6 Spread icing over biscuits. Refrigerate 3 hours or overnight.

passionfruit icing Sift icing sugar into small heatproof bowl; stir in butter, passionfruit and enough of the water to make a thick paste. Place bowl over small saucepan of simmering water; stir until icing is spreadable.

prep + cook time
30 minutes (+ refrigeration)
makes 12

chocolate peanut slice

When beating sugar into the egg white, beat only until combined; the sugar will not dissolve at this stage. Slice can be stored in an airtight container in the refrigerator for a week.

1½ sheets shortcrust pastry
⅔ cup (220g) raspberry jam
3 egg whites
1½ cups (330g) caster (superfine) sugar
1 cup (110g) plain cake crumbs
⅓ cup (35g) cocoa powder
1 teaspoon vanilla extract
1¾ cups (250g) roasted unsalted peanuts
2 teaspoons icing (confectioners') sugar

1 Preheat oven to 200°C/400°F.
2 Place pastry sheets on flat oven tray, prick all over with a fork; bake about 10 minutes or until pastry is browned lightly and almost cooked through. Place hot pastry pieces, side-by-side, on flat surface; using base of a 20cm x 30cm (8-inch x 12-inch) rectangular pan as a guide, cut pastry to fit pan. Grease and line base and sides of pan; place trimmed pastry into base of pan. Spread pastry evenly with jam.
3 Reduce oven to 180°C/350°F.
4 Beat egg whites in small bowl with electric mixer until firm peaks form. Beat in sugar in three batches (see notes). Stir in cake crumbs, sifted cocoa, extract then nuts. Spread nut mixture evenly over jam.
5 Bake slice about 40 minutes. Cool in pan before cutting. Dust with sifted icing sugar before serving.

prep + cook time
1 hour (+ cooling)
makes 30

apple streusel slice

Slice will keep in an airtight container in the refrigerator for up to 3 days

220g (7 ounces) unsalted butter, softened
1 cup (220g) caster (superfine) sugar
2 egg yolks
1⅓ cups (200g) plain (all-purpose) flour
½ cup (75g) self-raising flour
2 tablespoons custard powder
4 large apples (800g), sliced thinly
1 tablespoon honey
1 teaspoon finely grated lemon rind

streusel topping
½ cup (75g) plain (all-purpose) flour
¼ cup (35g) self-raising flour
⅓ cup (75g) firmly packed light brown sugar
½ teaspoon ground cinnamon
90g (3 ounces) unsalted butter, chopped coarsely

1 Make streusel topping.
2 Preheat oven to 180°C/350°F. Grease 20cm x 30cm (8-inch x 12-inch) rectangular pan; line base and long sides with baking paper, extending paper 5cm (2 inches) over sides.
3 Beat butter, sugar and egg yolks in small bowl with electric mixer until light and fluffy, transfer to large bowl; stir in sifted flours and custard powder. Press mixture into pan.
4 Bake 25 minutes. Cool in pan 15 minutes.
5 Meanwhile, cook apple, honey and rind, covered, in medium saucepan, stirring occasionally, about 5 minutes or until apples are tender. Remove from heat; drain, cool 15 minutes.
6 Spread apple mixture over base; coarsely grate streusel topping over apple.
7 Bake slice about 20 minutes. Cool slice in pan.
streusel topping Process ingredients until combined. Wrap in plastic; freeze 1 hour or until firm.

prep + cook time
1 hour (+ freezing & cooling)
makes 12

chocolate brownie slice

125g (4 ounces) butter, chopped coarsely
185g (6 ounces) dark eating (semi-sweet) chocolate, chopped coarsely
½ cup (110g) caster (superfine) sugar
2 eggs
1¼ cups (185g) plain (all-purpose) flour
155g (5 ounces) white eating chocolate, chopped coarsely
90g (3 ounces) milk eating chocolate, chopped coarsely

1 Preheat oven to 180°C/350°F. Grease deep 20cm (8-inch) square cake pan; line base with baking paper, extending paper 5cm (2 inches) over sides.
2 Stir butter and dark chocolate in medium saucepan over low heat until smooth. Remove from heat; cool 10 minutes.
3 Stir in sugar and eggs, then sifted flour, white chocolate and milk chocolate. Spread mixture into pan.
4 Bake slice about 35 minutes. Cool in pan.

prep + cook time 1 hour
makes 25

fruit mince slice

Use white (granulated) sugar instead of the demerara, if you like. Slice can be stored in an airtight container for up to a week.

1½ cups (225g) plain (all-purpose) flour
1¼ cups (185g) self-raising flour
155g (5 ounces) cold butter, chopped
1 tablespoon golden syrup or treacle
1 egg
⅓ cup (80ml) milk, approximately
2 teaspoons milk, extra
1 tablespoon demerara sugar

fruit mince
500g (1 pound) mixed dried fruit, chopped coarsely
½ cup (125ml) water
½ cup (110g) firmly packed dark brown sugar
1 tablespoon orange marmalade
2 teaspoons finely grated orange rind
2 tablespoons orange juice

1 Make fruit mince.
2 Grease 20cm x 30cm (8-inch x 12-inch) rectangular pan; line base and long sides with baking paper, extending paper 5cm (2 inches) over sides.
3 Sift flours into large bowl; rub in butter until mixture is crumbly. Stir in combined syrup and egg with enough milk to make a firm dough. Knead dough gently on floured surface until smooth. Refrigerate 30 minutes.
4 Preheat oven to 200°C/400°F.
5 Divide dough in half. Roll one half between sheets of baking paper until large enough to cover base of pan; press into pan. Spread fruit mince over dough.
6 Roll remaining dough between sheets of baking paper until large enough to cover fruit mince; place on top of fruit mince, trim to fit. Brush with extra milk; sprinkle with sugar.
7 Bake slice about 20 minutes. Cool in pan before cutting.

fruit mince Cook ingredients in medium saucepan, stirring, over medium heat, about 10 minutes or until thick. Cool.

prep + cook time 50 minutes
(+ refrigeration & cooling)
makes 24

white chocolate and berry cheesecake slice

It is fine to use just one 300ml carton of cream for this recipe.

250g (8 ounces) butternut snap biscuits
2 teaspoons gelatine
¼ cup (60ml) boiling water
375g (12 ounces) softened cream cheese
⅓ cup (75g) caster (superfine) sugar
1¼ cups (310ml) pouring cream
185g (6 ounces) white eating chocolate, melted
125g (4 ounces) frozen mixed berries
90g (3 ounces) frozen mixed berries, extra

1 Grease deep 20cm (8-inch) square loose-based cake pan.
2 Place biscuits in base of pan.
3 Sprinkle gelatine over water in small heatproof jug; stand jug in small saucepan of simmering water, stir until gelatine dissolves. Cool 5 minutes.
4 Meanwhile, beat cream cheese and sugar in small bowl with electric mixer until smooth; beat in cream. Stir in gelatine mixture, chocolate and berries. Pour filling into pan; sprinkle with extra berries.
5 Refrigerate slice 3 hours or overnight.

prep + cook time
30 minutes (+ refrigeration)
makes 20

lime and coconut slice

240g (7½ ounces) plain sweet biscuits
½ cup (120g) sweetened condensed milk
90g (3 ounces) unsalted butter, chopped
1 teaspoon finely grated lime rind
1 tablespoon lime juice
½ cup (40g) shredded coconut

lime icing
2 cups (320g) icing (confectioners') sugar
15g (½ ounce) unsalted butter, melted
2 tablespoons lime juice

1 Grease 20cm x 30cm (8-inch x 12-inch) rectangular pan; line base and long sides with baking paper, extending paper 5cm (2 inches) over sides.
2 Process 185g (6 ounces) of the biscuits until fine; chop remaining biscuits coarsely.
3 Stir condensed milk and butter in small saucepan over medium heat until smooth.
4 Combine processed and chopped biscuits, rind, juice and coconut in medium bowl. Add condensed milk mixture; stir to combine.
5 Press mixture firmly into pan. Refrigerate 30 minutes or until firm.
6 Meanwhile, make lime icing.
7 Spread icing over slice. Refrigerate 30 minutes or until firm.

lime icing Sift icing sugar into small heatproof bowl; stir in butter, juice and enough water to make a thick paste. Place bowl over small saucepan of simmering water, stir until icing is spreadable.

prep + cook time
25 minutes (+ refrigeration)
makes 24

slices

bakewell slice

Slice can be stored in an airtight container for up to a week.

- 155g (5 ounces) unsalted butter, softened
- ¼ cup (55g) caster (superfine) sugar
- 2 egg yolks
- 1½ cups (225g) plain (all-purpose) flour
- ¾ cup (90g) ground almonds
- ¾ cup (240g) strawberry jam

almond filling
- 185g (6 ounces) unsalted butter, softened
- 1 teaspoon finely grated lemon rind
- ¾ cup (165g) caster (superfine) sugar
- 3 eggs
- 1¼ cups (150g) ground almonds
- ¼ cup (35g) plain (all-purpose) flour

lemon icing
- 2 cups (320g) icing (confectioners') sugar
- ¼ cup (60ml) lemon juice, approximately

1 Beat butter, sugar and egg yolks in small bowl with electric mixer until combined. Stir in sifted flour and ground almonds, in two batches. Knead pastry gently on floured surface until smooth. Wrap in plastic; refrigerate 30 minutes.
2 Make almond filling.
3 Meanwhile, preheat oven to 200°C/400°F.
4 Grease 20cm x 30cm (8-inch x 12-inch) rectangular pan; line base and long sides with baking paper, extending paper 5cm (2 inches) over sides. Roll out pastry between sheets of baking paper until large enough to line pan; press into base and sides, trim edge. Spread jam then almond filling evenly over base.
5 Bake about 30 minutes. Cool in pan.
6 Make lemon icing.
7 Spread lemon icing over slice; stand at room temperature until icing is set.

almond filling Beat butter, rind and sugar in small bowl with electric mixer until light and fluffy. Beat in eggs, one at a time. Stir in ground almonds and sifted flour.
lemon icing Sift icing sugar into small bowl; stir in enough of the juice until icing is spreadable.

prep + cook time
1 hour 10 minutes
(+ refrigeration & standing)
makes 32

hedgehog slice

We used plain sweet shortbread biscuits.

395g (14 ounces) canned sweetened condensed milk
90g (3 ounces) unsalted butter, chopped coarsely
185g (6 ounces) dark eating (semi-sweet) chocolate, chopped coarsely
250g (8 ounces) plain sweet biscuits
⅔ cup (90g) roasted hazelnuts
⅔ cup (110g) sultanas

1 Grease 20cm x 30cm (8-inch x 12-inch) rectangular pan; line base and long sides with baking paper, extending paper 5cm (2 inches) over sides.
2 Stir condensed milk and butter in medium saucepan over medium heat until smooth. Remove from heat; add chocolate, stir until smooth.
3 Break biscuits into small pieces; place in large bowl with nuts and sultanas. Stir in chocolate mixture.
4 Press mixture firmly into pan. Refrigerate 2 hours or until firm.

prep + cook time
20 minutes (+ refrigeration)
makes 20

blueberry, lime and passionfruit slice

6 egg whites
1½ cups (180g) ground almonds
1½ cups (240g) icing (confectioners') sugar
¼ cup (35g) plain (all-purpose) flour
¼ cup (35g) self-raising flour
½ cup (40g) desiccated coconut
155g (5 ounces) butter, melted
2 teaspoons finely grated lime rind
155g (5 ounces) fresh or frozen blueberries
¼ cup (60ml) passionfruit pulp

1 Preheat oven to 180°C/350°F. Grease 20cm x 30cm (8-inch x 12-inch) rectangular pan; line base and long sides with baking paper, extending paper 5cm (2 inches) over sides.
2 Whisk egg whites in large bowl until frothy; stir in ground almonds, icing sugar, sifted flours, coconut, butter and rind. Pour mixture into pan; sprinkle with berries, drizzle with passionfruit.
3 Bake slice about 1¼ hours; stand slice in pan 10 minutes before turning, top-side up, onto wire rack to cool. Cut into rectangles; dust with sifted icing sugar to serve.

prep + cook time
1 hour 40 minutes
makes 16

choc-peanut caramel slice

Always use a premium-quality eating chocolate when baking rather than compound or any labelled light or low fat. The important thing is to use "real" chocolate, which means that it has to contain cocoa butter. If cocoa butter isn't shown on the packaging, don't buy it.

125g (4 ounces) butter, chopped
1 cup (220g) caster (superfine) sugar
395g (12½ ounces) canned sweetened condensed milk
1 cup (140g) roasted unsalted peanuts
200g (6½ ounces) dark eating (semi-sweet) chocolate, chopped coarsely
20g (¾ ounce) butter, extra

1 Grease deep 20cm (8-inch) square cake pan. Fold 40cm (16-inch) piece of foil lengthways into thirds; place foil strip over base and up two sides of pan (this will help lift the slice out of the pan). Line base with baking paper.
2 Stir butter, sugar and milk in medium heavy-based saucepan over medium heat, without boiling, until sugar dissolves. Bring to the boil; boil, stirring constantly, about 10 minutes or until caramel mixture becomes a dark-honey colour and starts to come away from the base and side of pan.
3 Working quickly and carefully (the mixture is very hot), pour caramel into pan; smooth with metal spatula. Press nuts into caramel with spatula. Cool 20 minutes.
4 Stir chocolate and extra butter in small heatproof bowl over small saucepan of simmering water until smooth; spread chocolate mixture over slice. Refrigerate until set. Use foil strip to lift slice from pan before cutting into squares.

prep + cook time 40 minutes (+ cooling & refrigeration)
makes 40

double-chocolate slice

Slice can be stored in an airtight container for up to a week.

125g (4 ounces) butter, chopped coarsely
1 cup (220g) firmly packed dark brown sugar
185g (6 ounces) dark eating (semi-sweet) chocolate
1¼ cups (110g) rolled oats
¾ cup (75g) coarsely chopped walnuts
1 egg
¾ cup (110g) plain (all-purpose) flour
¼ cup (35g) self-raising flour
½ teaspoon bicarbonate of soda (baking soda)
⅔ cup (130g) dark choc bits

1 Preheat oven to 160°C/325°F. Grease 20cm x 30cm (8-inch x 12-inch) rectangular pan; line base and long sides with baking paper, extending paper 5cm (2 inches) over sides.
2 Melt butter in medium saucepan over low heat. Remove from heat; stir in sugar until smooth.
3 Coarsely chop half the dark eating chocolate.
4 Stir oats and nuts into butter mixture, then egg, sifted dry ingredients, chopped chocolate and choc bits. Spread mixture evenly into pan.
5 Bake slice about 30 minutes. Cover hot slice with foil; cool.
6 Melt remaining dark eating chocolate. Turn slice, top-side-up, onto wire rack; drizzle with melted chocolate. Stand slice at room temperature until set before cutting.

prep + cook time 45 minutes (+ cooling & standing)
makes 30

apple and prune slice

4 medium apples (600g)
¾ cup (135g) coarsely chopped seeded prunes
2½ cups (625ml) water
½ teaspoon each ground cinnamon and ground nutmeg
2 tablespoons ground hazelnuts
2 sheets shortcrust pastry
1 tablespoon caster (superfine) sugar

1 Peel and core apples; slice thinly. Place apples, prunes and the water in medium saucepan; bring to the boil. Reduce heat; simmer, covered, 10 minutes or until apples are just tender. Drain well; cool 15 minutes.
2 Combine spices and ground hazelnuts in medium bowl; gently stir in apple mixture.
3 Preheat oven to 200°C/400°F. Grease 20cm x 30cm (8-inch x 12-inch) lamington pan; line base with baking paper.
4 Roll one pastry sheet large enough to cover base of pan; place in pan, trim edges. Line pastry with baking paper, fill with dried beans or rice; bake 15 minutes. Remove paper and beans; bake further 5 minutes. Spread apple mixture over pastry.
5 Roll remaining pastry sheet large enough to fit pan; place over apple filling. Brush pastry with a little water, sprinkle with sugar; score pastry in crosshatch pattern.
6 Bake slice about 45 minutes. Cool in pan; cut into squares.

prep + cook time
1 hour 30 minutes (+ cooling)
makes 24

macadamia caramel slice

Slice can be stored, refrigerated in an airtight container, for up to 4 days.

⅓ cup (50g) self-raising flour
⅓ cup (50g) plain (all-purpose) flour
¾ cup (165g) firmly packed light brown sugar
⅔ cup (50g) desiccated coconut
90g (3 ounces) butter, melted
395g (14 ounces) canned sweetened condensed milk
30g (1 ounce) butter, extra
2 tablespoons golden syrup or treacle
¾ cup (105g) coarsely chopped macadamias, roasted
500g (1 pound) white eating chocolate, chopped coarsely
1 tablespoon vegetable oil
pink food colouring

1 Preheat oven to 180°C/350°F. Grease 20cm x 30cm (8-inch x 12-inch) lamington pan; line with baking paper, extending paper 5cm (2 inch) over long sides.
2 Sift flours and sugar into medium bowl, mix in coconut and butter; press mixture evenly over base of pan. Bake 15 minutes.
3 Meanwhile, stir condensed milk, extra butter and syrup in small saucepan over medium heat about 15 minutes or until caramel mixture is golden brown.
4 Working quickly, pour caramel over base; smooth with metal spatula. Press nuts into caramel with spatula. Bake 10 minutes; cool.
5 Stir half the chocolate and half the oil in small saucepan over low heat until smooth. Pour chocolate mixture over caramel. Refrigerate 30 minutes.
6 Stir remaining chocolate and remaining oil in same cleaned pan over low heat until smooth; tint with pink food colouring. Pour pink chocolate over white chocolate. Refrigerate 2 hours. Stand slice at room temperature at least 30 minutes before cutting into squares with sharp knife.

prep + cook time 50 minutes (+ cooling & refrigeration)
makes 60

choc-cherry macaroon slice

3 egg whites
½ cup (110g) caster (superfine) sugar
100g (3 ounces) dark eating (semi-sweet) chocolate, grated coarsely
¼ cup (35g) plain (all-purpose) flour
1⅓ cups (95g) shredded coconut, toasted
¾ cup (150g) glacé cherries, chopped coarsely
50g (1½ ounces) dark eating (semi-sweet) chocolate, melted

1 Preheat oven to 150°C/300°F. Grease base of 20cm x 30cm (8-inch x 12-inch) rectangular pan; line base and two long sides with baking paper, extending paper 2.5cm (1 inch) over long sides.
2 Beat egg whites in small bowl with electric mixer until soft peaks form; gradually add sugar, beating until dissolved between additions.
3 Fold in grated chocolate, flour, coconut and cherries. Spread mixture into pan.
4 Bake slice about 45 minutes. Cool to room temperature in pan.
5 Drizzle slice with melted chocolate; refrigerate until set before cutting.

prep + cook time
1 hour (+ cooling & refrigeration)
makes 16

lemon meringue slice

It is fine to use just one 300ml carton of cream for this recipe.

90g (3 ounces) butter, softened
2 tablespoons caster (superfine) sugar
1 egg
1 cup (150g) plain (all-purpose) flour
¼ cup (80g) apricot jam

lemon filling
2 eggs
2 egg yolks
½ cup (110g) caster (superfine) sugar
1¼ cups (310ml) pouring cream
1 tablespoon finely grated lemon rind
2 tablespoons lemon juice

meringue
3 egg whites
¾ cup (165g) caster (superfine) sugar

1 Preheat oven to 200°C/400°F. Grease base of 20cm x 30cm (8-inch x 12-inch) lamington pan; line base and two long sides with baking paper, extending paper 2.5cm (1 inch) over long sides.
2 Beat butter, sugar and egg in small bowl with electric mixer until pale in colour; stir in sifted flour, in two batches. Press dough over base of pan; prick several times with fork.
3 Bake base about 15 minutes or until browned lightly. Cool 20 minutes; spread base with jam.
4 Reduce oven to 170°C/340°F.
5 Make lemon filling; pour over base.
6 Bake about 35 minutes or until set; cool 20 minutes. Roughen surface of filling with fork.
7 Increase oven to 220°C/425°F.
8 Make meringue; spread evenly over filling.
9 Bake slice about 3 minutes or until browned lightly. Cool in pan 20 minutes before cutting.
lemon filling Whisk ingredients in medium bowl until combined.
meringue Beat egg whites in small bowl with electric mixer until soft peaks form; gradually add sugar, beating until sugar dissolves.

prep + cook time
1 hour 20 minutes (+ cooling)
makes 16

dutch ginger and almond slice

1¾ cups (260g) plain (all-purpose) flour
1 cup (220g) caster (superfine) sugar
⅔ cup (150g) coarsely chopped glacé ginger
½ cup (80g) blanched almonds, chopped coarsely
1 egg
185g (6 ounces) butter, melted
2 teaspoons icing (confectioners') sugar

1 Preheat oven to 180°C/350°F. Grease 20cm x 30cm (8-inch x 12-inch) rectangular pan; line base and long sides with baking paper, extending paper 5cm (2 inches) over sides.
2 Combine sifted flour, sugar, ginger, nuts and egg in medium bowl; stir in butter. Press mixture into pan.
3 Bake slice about 35 minutes. Stand slice in pan 10 minutes before lifting onto wire rack to cool. Dust with sifted icing sugar before cutting.

prep + cook time 50 minutes
makes 20

glossary

allspice also called pimento or jamaican pepper; it tastes like a combination of cumin, nutmeg, clove and cinnamon. It is available whole (pea-sized berry) or ground.

almonds
blanched whole nuts with brown skins removed.
flaked paper thin almond slices.
ground also called almond meal; nuts are powdered to a coarse flour-like texture.

baking paper also called parchment, is a silicone-coated paper that is primarily used for lining baking pans and oven trays so cakes and biscuits won't stick, making removal easy.

baking powder a raising agent consisting mainly of two parts cream of tartar to one part bicarbonate of soda (baking soda).

bicarbonate of soda (baking soda) a raising agent used in baking.

biscuits also known as cookies.
butternut snap crunchy cookie made with golden syrup, oats and coconut.
chocolate wheaten wheatmeal-based biscuit, topped with milk or dark chocolate.
lattice an open-weave square-shaped biscuit. These flaky pastry biscuits are made from flour, oil, sugar and milk powder. The dough is gently rolled into very fine sheets, just like flaky pastry, and is then glazed with a light sprinkling of sugar before being baked until puffed and golden.
shortbread a pale golden, crumbly, buttery-tasting cookie made of butter, sugar and flour.

butter use salted or unsalted (sweet) butter; 125g is equal to one stick (4 ounces) of butter.

buttermilk originally the term given to the slightly sour liquid left after butter was churned from cream, today it is made similarly to yogurt. Sold alongside fresh milk products in supermarkets. Despite the implication of its name, buttermilk is low in fat.

capers the grey-green buds of a warm climate (usually Mediterranean) shrub, sold either dried and salted or pickled in a vinegar brine; baby capers are also available both in brine or dried in salt.

cardamom a spice native to India and used extensively in its cuisine; can be purchased in pod, seed or ground form. Has a distinctive aromatic, sweetly rich flavour.

cheese
cream commonly known as Philadelphia or Philly, a soft cows'-milk cheese with a fat content of at least 33%. Sold at supermarkets in bulk or in smaller-sized packages.
mascarpone an Italian fresh cultured-cream product made in much the same way as yogurt. Whiteish to creamy yellow in colour, with a buttery-rich, luscious texture. Soft, creamy and spreadable, it is used in Italian desserts and as an accompaniment to fresh fruit.

chocolate
dark eating (semi-sweet) also known as luxury chocolate; made of a high percentage of cocoa liquor and cocoa butter, and a little added sugar.
freckles small chocolate discs topped with hundreds and thousands.
milk eating the most popular eating chocolate, mild and very sweet; similar to dark with the difference being the addition of milk solids.
peppermint cream a confectionery with a peppermint fondant centre that is covered in dark chocolate.
peppermint crisp a chocolate bar with a crisp peppermint centre covered with dark chocolate.
white eating contains no cocoa solids but derives its sweet flavour from cocoa butter. Is very sensitive to heat, so watch carefully when melting.
chocolate hazelnut spread we use Nutella in this book.

cinnamon dried inner bark of the shoots of the cinnamon tree; available in stick (quill) or ground form.

glossary

cloves dried flower buds of a tropical tree; can be used whole or in ground form. Has a distinctively pungent and 'spicy' scent and flavour.
cocoa powder also called cocoa; dried, unsweetened, roasted then ground cocoa beans (cacao seeds).
coconut
desiccated concentrated, dried, unsweetened and finely shredded coconut flesh.
flaked dried flaked coconut flesh.
shredded unsweetened thin strips of dried coconut flesh.
cornflour (cornstarch) used as a thickening agent. Available as 100% corn (maize) and wheaten cornflour.
cream
pouring also called fresh or pure cream. It has no additives and a minimum fat content 35%.
thick (double) a dolloping cream with a minimum fat content of 45%.
thickened a whipping cream containing a thickener; has a minimum fat content 35%.
cream of tartar the acid ingredient in baking powder; added to confectionery mixtures to help prevent sugar from crystallising. Keeps frostings creamy and improves volume when beating egg whites.
crème fraîche a mature, naturally fermented cream (minimum fat content 35%) with a velvety texture and slightly tangy, nutty flavour. A French variation of sour cream, it can boil without curdling and can be used in sweet and savoury dishes.
cucumber, lebanese short, slender and thin-skinned. Probably the most popular variety because of its tender, edible skin, tiny, yielding seeds, and sweet, fresh and flavoursome taste.
custard powder instant mixture used to make pouring custard; it is similar to North American instant pudding mixes.
dill also called dill weed; used fresh or dried, in seed form or ground. Adds an anise/celery sweet flavour to food. Distinctive feathery, frond-like fresh leaves are grassier and more subtle than the dried version of the seeds (which slightly resemble caraway in flavour).
dried cranberries dried sweetened cranberries; commercially labelled as craisins.
eggs if recipes call for raw or barely cooked eggs, exercise caution if there is a salmonella problem in your area, particularly for children and pregnant women.
flour
plain (all-purpose) made from wheat.
rice a very fine flour made from ground white rice.
self-raising plain flour that has been sifted with baking powder in the proportion of 1 cup flour to 2 teaspoons baking powder.
wholemeal milled from whole wheat grain (bran, germ and endosperm). Available as plain or self-raising.
food colouring dyes that can be used to change the colour of various foods. These dyes can be eaten and do not change the taste to a noticeable extent.
gelatine if using gelatine leaves, 3 teaspoons of powdered gelatine (8g or one sachet) is roughly equivalent to four gelatine leaves.
ginger
fresh also called green or root ginger; the thick gnarled root of a tropical plant. Can be kept, peeled, covered with dry sherry in a jar and refrigerated, or frozen in an airtight container.
glacé fresh ginger root preserved in sugar syrup; crystallised ginger (sweetened with cane sugar) can be substituted if rinsed with warm water and dried before using.
ground also called powdered ginger; used as a flavouring in cakes, pies and puddings but cannot be substituted for fresh ginger.
glacé fruit fruit such as peaches, pineapple, orange and citron that have been preserved by boiling in a heavy sugar syrup.

glossary

glucose syrup also called liquid glucose; a sugar syrup made from starches such as wheat and corn.
golden syrup a by-product of refined sugarcane; pure maple syrup or honey can be substituted.
hazelnuts also called filberts; plump, grape-size, rich, sweet nut with a brown inedible skin that is removed by rubbing heated nuts together vigorously in a tea-towel.
ground also called hazelnut meal; hazelnuts ground into a coarse or fine powder.
hundreds and thousands tiny sugar-syrup-coated sugar crystals that come in a variety of colours.
jam also called preserve or conserve; most often made from fruit.
liqueurs/spirits
coconut-flavoured we used Malibu, but you can use your favourite coconut-flavoured liqueur.
hazelnut-flavoured we used Frangelico but you can use your favourite hazelnut-flavoured liqueur.
limoncello Italian lemon-flavoured liqueur; originally made from the juice and peel of lemons grown along the Amalfi coast.
rum we prefer to use an underproof rum in baking because of its more subtle flavour; however, you can use an overproof rum and still get satisfactory results.

maple syrup distilled from the sap of sugar maple trees. Most often eaten with pancakes or waffles, but also used as an ingredient in baking or in preparing desserts. Maple-flavoured syrup or pancake syrup is not an adequate substitute for the real thing.
marmalade a preserve, usually based on citrus fruit and its rind, cooked with sugar until the mixture has an intense flavour and thick consistency. Orange, lemon and lime are some of the commercially prepared varieties available.
mayonnaise we use whole-egg mayonnaise in our recipes unless stated otherwise.
milk
caramel top 'n' fill a canned milk product made of condensed milk that has been boiled to a caramel. Can be used straight from the can for cheesecakes, slices and tarts.
malted milk powder a combination of wheat flour, malt flour and milk, which are evaporated to give the powder its fine appearance and to make it easily absorbable in liquids.
sweetened condensed milk from which 60% of the water has been removed; the remaining milk is then sweetened with sugar.
mixed peel candied citrus peel.

mixed spice a blend of ground spices usually consisting of cinnamon, allspice and nutmeg.
mustard, dijon also called french. Pale brown, creamy, distinctively flavoured, fairly mild french mustard.
nutmeg a strong and pungent spice ground from the dried nut of an evergreen tree native to Indonesia. Usually found ground but the flavour is more intense from a whole nut, available from spice shops, so it's best to grate your own.
oil, vegetable any of a number of oils sourced from plant rather than animal fats.
orange blossom water also called orange flower water; a concentrated flavouring made from orange blossoms. Available from Middle-Eastern food stores, some supermarkets and delis. Can't be substituted with citrus flavourings as the taste is completely different.
pastry sheets packaged ready-rolled sheets of frozen puff and shortcrust (sweet and savoury) pastry, available from supermarkets.
peanut butter peanuts ground to a paste; available in crunchy and smooth varieties.
peanuts not, in fact, a nut but the pod of a legume; also called ground nut.

glossary

pepitas are the pale green kernels of dried pumpkin seeds; they can be bought plain or salted.

pine nuts also known as pignoli; not a nut but a small, cream-coloured kernel from pine cones. They are best roasted before use to bring out the flavour.

pistachios green, delicately flavoured nuts inside hard off-white shells. Available salted or unsalted in their shells; you can also get them shelled.

pomegranate dark-red, leathery-skinned fresh fruit about the size of an orange, filled with hundreds of seeds wrapped in an edible lucent-crimson pulp having a unique tangy sweet-sour flavour.

poppy seeds small, dried, bluish-grey seeds of the poppy plant, with a crunchy texture and a nutty flavour. Can be purchased whole or ground in delicatessens and most supermarkets.

quince yellow-skinned fruit with hard texture and astringent, tart taste; eaten cooked or as a preserve. Long, slow cooking makes the flesh a deep rose pink.

rhubarb a plant with long, green-red stalks; becomes sweet and edible when cooked.

rolled oats oat groats (oats that have been husked) steamed-softened, flattened, dried and packaged as a cereal product.

rosewater distilled from rose petals, and used in the Middle East, North Africa and India to flavour desserts. Don't confuse with rose essence, which is more concentrated.

semolina coarsely ground flour milled from durum wheat; the flour used in making gnocchi, pasta and couscous.

star anise a dried star-shaped pod whose seeds have an astringent aniseed flavour; commonly used to flavour stocks and marinades.

sugar
caster (superfine) also called finely granulated table sugar.
dark brown a moist, dark brown sugar with a rich, distinctive, full flavour coming from natural molasses syrup.
demerara a granulated, golden coloured sugar with a distinctive rich flavour; often used to sweeten coffee.
icing (confectioners') also known as powdered sugar; granulated sugar crushed together with a little added cornflour (cornstarch).
icing pure (confectioners') also known as powdered sugar, but has no added cornflour (cornstarch).
light brown an extremely soft, finely granulated sugar retaining molasses for its characteristic colour and flavour.
white (granulated) also known as crystal sugar; a coarse, granulated table sugar.

treacle a concentrated, refined sugar syrup with a distinctive flavour and dark black colour.

vanilla
bean dried, long, thin pod from a tropical golden orchid; the minuscule black seeds inside the bean are used to impart a luscious vanilla flavour in baking and desserts. Place a whole bean in a jar of sugar to make the vanilla sugar; a bean can be used three or four times.
extract obtained from vanilla beans infused in water; a non-alcoholic version of essence.

watercress one of the cress family, a large group of peppery greens used raw in salads, dips and sandwiches, or cooked in soups. Highly perishable, so it must be used as soon as possible after purchase.

wheat germ the germ is where the seed germinates to form the sprout that becomes wheat. It has a nutty flavour and is very oily, causing it to turn rancid quickly, so is usually removed during milling. Available from health-food stores and supermarkets.

yogurt we use plain full-cream yogurt in our recipes unless stated otherwise.

conversion chart

measures

One Australian metric measuring cup holds about 250ml; one Australian metric tablespoon holds 20ml; one Australian metric teaspoon holds 5ml. The difference between one country's measuring cups and another's is within a two- or three-teaspoon variance, and will not affect your cooking results. North America, New Zealand and the United Kingdom use a 15ml tablespoon.

All cup and spoon measurements are level. The most accurate way of measuring dry ingredients is to weigh them. When measuring liquids, use a clear glass or plastic jug with the metric markings.

We use large eggs with an average weight of 60g.

The imperial measurements used in these recipes are approximate only.

dry measures

METRIC	IMPERIAL
15g	½oz
30g	1oz
60g	2oz
90g	3oz
125g	4oz (¼lb)
155g	5oz
185g	6oz
220g	7oz
250g	8oz (½lb)
280g	9oz
315g	10oz
345g	11oz
375g	12oz (¾lb)
410g	13oz
440g	14oz
470g	15oz
500g	16oz (1lb)
750g	24oz (1½lb)
1kg	32oz (2lb)

liquid measures

METRIC	IMPERIAL
30ml	1 fluid oz
60ml	2 fluid oz
100ml	3 fluid oz
125ml	4 fluid oz
150ml	5 fluid oz (¼ pint/1 gill)
190ml	6 fluid oz
250ml	8 fluid oz
300ml	10 fluid oz (½ pint)
500ml	16 fluid oz
600ml	20 fluid oz (1 pint)
1000ml (1 litre)	1¾ pints

length measures

3mm	⅛in
6mm	¼in
1cm	½in
2cm	¾in
2.5cm	1in
5cm	2in
6cm	2½in
8cm	3in
10cm	4in
13cm	5in
15cm	6in
18cm	7in
20cm	8in
23cm	9in
25cm	10in
28cm	11in
30cm	12in (1ft)

oven temperatures

The oven temperatures in this book are for conventional ovens; if you have a fan-forced oven, decrease the temperature by 10-20 degrees.

	°C (CELSIUS)	°F (FAHRENHEIT)
Very slow	120	250
Slow	150	300
Moderately slow	160	325
Moderate	180	350
Moderately hot	200	400
Hot	220	425
Very hot	240	475

index

A
allspice 248
almond 248
  almond carrot cake 126
  almond honey spice cake 133
  amaretti 152
  chicken and almond sandwiches 10
  coffee almond biscuits 196
  dutch ginger and almond slice 247
  filling 50
  greek almond crescents 140
  orange almond victoria sponge 97
  rhubarb and almond cakes 82
amaretti 152
apple and prune slice 239
apple
  apple cinnamon tea loaves 78
  apple streusel slice 219

B
bakewell slice 228
baking paper 248
baking powder 248
baklava twists 163
berry cream 109
berry cream roulade 109
berry cupcakes, gluten-free 86
bicarbonate of soda 248
biscuits 248
  amaretti 152
  baklava twists 163
  brandy snaps 167
  chocolate caramel shortbread cookies 164
  chocolate chip cookies 143
  chocolate chunk and raspberry cookies 144
  chocolate french macaroons 183
  chocolate lace crisps 200

(*biscuits* continued)
  chocolate wheaties 156
  coconut chocolate crunchies 175
  coconut french macaroons 184
  coffee almond 196
  greek almond crescents 140
  hazelnut moments with choc berry filling 172
  hazelnut pinwheels 192
  jam drops 147
  lime and ginger kisses 171
  linzer 195
  malted milk flowers 155
  melting moments 160
  mocha vanilla twists 148
  monte carlos 188
  passionfruit cream 191
  passionfruit meringue kisses 179
  pistachio, white chocolate and honey french macaroons 180
  refrigerator slice-and-bake cookies 151
  spicy fruit mince pillows 168
  strawberry french macaroons 187
  traditional shortbread 159
  vanilla bean thins 199
  wagonettes 176
black forest gateaux 77
blueberry, lime and passionfruit slice 232
boiled whisky fruit cake 125
brandy snaps 167
brown sugar sponge 114
butter 248
butter cream 160
buttermilk 248

C
cakes, big
  almond carrot 126

(*cakes, big* continued)
  almond honey spice 133
  berry cream roulade 109
  boiled whisky fruit 125
  brown sugar sponge 114
  chocolate and pecan torte 98
  chocolate banana 113
  chocolate mud cake with chilli cherries 130
  fresh ginger cake with golden ginger cream 117
  lemon 118
  lemon and lime white chocolate mud 110
  lime and poppy seed syrup 105
  muscat prune shortcake 129
  orange almond victoria sponge 97
  pink velvet 94
  pistachio buttercake with orange honey syrup 102
  quince and blackberry crumble 137
  raspberry cream sponge 101
  spices of the orient teacake 122
  tiramisu roulade 106
  upside-down toffee date and banana 121
  whipped cream cake with caramel icing 134
cakes, little
  apple cinnamon tea loaves 78
  black forest gateaux 77
  carrot 74
  ginger powder puffs with orange cream 89
  gluten-free berry cupcakes 86
  jelly cakes with berry cream 90
  madeleines 73
  mini chocolate hazelnut 81
  mini sponge rolls 70

index

(*cakes, little* continued)
    passionfruit curd sponge 85
    rhubarb and almond 82
capers 248
caramel butter, whipped 28
caramel icing 134
caramel tarts 66
cardamom 248
carrot cakes 74
cheese 248
cherry bakewell tarts 50
chicken and almond sandwiches 10
chicken and celery sandwiches 21
chilli cherries 130
chocolate 248
    choc berry filling 172
    choc-cherry macaroon slice 243
    choc nut and cornflake slice 211
    choc-peanut caramel slice 235
    chocolate and pecan torte 98
    chocolate banana cake 113
    chocolate brownie slice 220
    chocolate caramel shortbread cookies 164
    chocolate caramel slice 204
    chocolate chip cookies 143
    chocolate chunk and raspberry cookies 144
    chocolate french macaroons 183
    chocolate lace crisps 200
    chocolate mud cake with chilli cherries 130
    chocolate peanut slice 216
    chocolate wheaties 156
    coconut chocolate crunchies 175
    dark chocolate ganache 130, 183
    double chocolate slice 236
    fruity choc chip slice 208
    ganache 77, 98
    milk chocolate ganache 175
    mini chocolate hazelnut cakes 81
    tartlets 62
chocolate hazelnut spread 248
cinnamon 248
    cinnamon crumble 137

cloves 249
cocoa powder 249
coconut 249
    coconut french macaroons 184
    coconut ganache 110
    passionfruit curd and coconut tarts 57
coffee almond biscuits 196
coffee liqueur cream 106
cookies *see* biscuits
cream 249
cream cheese frosting 126
cream of tartar 249
creamy choc frosting 113
crème brûlée praline tarts 65
crème fraîche 249
cucumber, lebanese
    marinated cucumber sandwiches 13
curried egg sandwiches 14
custard cream 46
custard fruit flans 46
custard powder 249

D
date scones with whipped caramel butter 28
dill 249
dried cranberries 249
dutch ginger and almond slice 247

E
eggs 249
    curried egg sandwiches 14

F
fig and walnut friands 37
flans, custard fruit 46
flour 249
food colouring 249
fresh ginger cake with golden ginger cream 117
french macaroons
    chocolate 183
    coconut 184
    pistachio, white chocolate and honey 180
    strawberry 187

friands
    fig and walnut 37
    lemon and cranberry 41
    mandarin and poppy seed 38
    orange blossom 34
    pistachio and lime 42
frosting *see also* icing
    cream cheese 126
    creamy choc 113
    lemon cream cheese 74
    lemon mascarpone 118
    mascarpone 94
fruit mince 223
fruit mince slice 223
fruity choc chip slice 208

G
ganache
    chocolate 77, 98
    coconut 110
    dark chocolate 130, 183
    honeyed white chocolate 180
    milk chocolate 175
    whipped hazelnut 81
    white chocolate 184
gelatine 249
ginger 249
    dutch ginger and almond slice 247
    fresh ginger cake with golden ginger cream 117
    ginger powder puffs with orange cream 89
gingerbread scones with lemon glacé icing 31
glacé fruit 249
glacé icing 53
    lemon 31
    raspberry 101
glucose syrup 250
gluten-free berry cupcakes 86
golden ginger cream 117
golden syrup 250
greek almond crescents 140

H
hazelnuts 250
    hazelnut moments with choc berry filling 172

index

(*hazelnuts* continued)
   hazelnut pinwheels 192
   mini chocolate hazelnut cakes 81
   rich hazelnut slice 207
   whipped hazelnut ganache 81
hedgehog slice 231
honey cream, spiced 78
honey orange cream 133
honey syrup 34
honeyed white chocolate
   ganache 180
hundreds and thousands 250

I
icing *see also* frosting
   glacé 53
   lemon 228
   lemon glacé 31
   lime 227
   malt 155
   passionfruit 215
   raspberry glacé 101

J
jam 250
   jam drops 147
jelly cakes with berry cream 90
jelly, mixed berry 90

L
lattice slice with passionfruit icing 215
lemon
   cake 118
   glacé icing 31
   glaze 50
   icing 228
   lemon and cranberry friands 41
   lemon and lime white chocolate
      mud cake 110
   lemon cream cheese frosting 74
   lemon crème brûlée tarts 61
   lemon mascarpone frosting 118
   lemon meringue slice 244
lime
   icing 227
   lime and coconut slice 227
   lime and ginger kisses 171

(*lime* continued)
   lime and poppy seed syrup
      cake 105
   lime butter cream 171
   lime pepper aïoli 18
   pistachio and lime friands 42
   syrup 105
limoncello curd 49
limoncello meringue pies 49
linzer biscuits 195
liqueurs/spirits 250

M
macadamia caramel slice 240
macaroons, french
   chocolate 183
   coconut 184
   pistachio, white chocolate
      and honey 180
   strawberry 187
madeleines 73
malt icing 155
malted milk flowers 155
mandarin and poppy seed friands 38
maple syrup 250
marinated cucumber sandwiches 13
marmalade 250
mascarpone frosting 94
mayonnaise 250
melting moments 160
milk 250
mixed berry jelly 90
mixed peel 250
mixed spice 250
mocha vanilla twists 148
mock cream 53, 70
muscat prune shortcake 129
muscat prunes 129
mustard, dijon 250

N
neenish and pineapple tarts 53
nutmeg 250

O
oil, vegetable 250
orange almond victoria sponge 97

orange blossom friands 34
orange blossom water 250
orange cream 89
orange honey syrup 102

P
passionfruit
   butter 179
   cream 191
   curd 57, 85
   icing 215
   passionfruit cream biscuits 191
   passionfruit curd and coconut
      tarts 57
   passionfruit curd sponge
      cakes 85
   passionfruit meringue kisses 179
pastry 61, 62
pastry sheets 250
peanut butter 250
peanuts 250
   choc-peanut caramel slice 235
   chocolate peanut slice 216
pepitas 251
pies, limoncello meringue 49
pine nuts 251
pink velvet cake 94
pistachios 251
   pistachio and lime friands 42
   pistachio buttercake with
      orange honey syrup 102
   pistachio, white chocolate
      and honey french macaroons
      180
pomegranate 251
poppy seeds 251
portuguese custard tarts 58
praline 65, 114
prawn and lime pepper aïoli
   sandwiches 18

Q
quince 251
   poached 137
   quince and blackberry crumble
      cake 137

index

R
raspberries
 raspberry coconut slice 212
 raspberry cream sponge 101
 raspberry glacé icing 101
refrigerator slice-and-bake
 cookies 151
rhubarb 251
 poached 82
 rhubarb and almond cakes 82
 rhubarb frangipane tarts 54
rich hazelnut slice 207
rolled oats 251
rosewater 251

S
salmon and herbed cream cheese
 sandwiches 17
sandwiches
 chicken and almond 10
 chicken and celery 21
 curried egg 14
 marinated cucumber 13
 prawn and lime pepper aïoli 18
 salmon and herbed cream
  cheese 17
scones
 date scones with whipped
  caramel butter 28
 gingerbread scones with
  lemon glacé icing 31
 jam and cream, with 24
 vanilla bean 27
seafood
 prawn and lime pepper aïoli
  sandwiches 18
 salmon and herbed cream cheese
  sandwiches 17
semolina 251
shortbread, traditional 159
slices
 apple and prune 239
 apple streusel 219
 blueberry, lime and passionfruit
  232
 choc-cherry macaroon 243
 choc nut and cornflake 211

(*slices* continued)
 choc-peanut caramel 235
 chocolate brownie 220
 chocolate caramel 204
 chocolate peanut 216
 double chocolate 236
 dutch ginger and almond 247
 fruit mince 223
 fruity choc chip 208
 hedgehog 231
 lattice slice with passionfruit
  icing 215
 lemon meringue 244
 lime and coconut 227
 macadamia caramel 240
 raspberry coconut 212
 rich hazelnut 207
 white chocolate and berry
  cheesecake 224
spiced honey cream 78
spiced nuts 122
spiced syrup 133
spices of the orient teacake 122
spicy fruit mince pillows 168
sponge rolls, mini 70
star anise 251
strawberry french macaroons 187
streusel topping 219
sugar 251

T
tarts, little
 caramel 66
 cherry bakewell 50
 chocolate tartlets 62
 crème brûlée praline 65
 custard fruit flans 46
 lemon crème brûlée 61
 limoncello meringue pies 49
 neenish and pineapple 53
 passionfruit curd and coconut 57
 portuguese custard 58
 rhubarb frangipane 54
teacake, spices of the orient 122
tiramisu roulade 106
toffee 61

toffee date and banana cake,
 upside-down 121
traditional shortbread 159
treacle 251

U
upside-down toffee date and
 banana cake 121

V
vanilla 251
 vanilla bean scones 27
 vanilla bean thins 199

W
wagonettes 176
watercress 251
wheatgerm 251
whipped caramel butter 28
whipped cream cake with
 caramel icing 134
whipped hazelnut ganache 81
white chocolate
 ganache 184
 honeyed white chocolate
  ganache 180
 lemon and lime white chocolate
  mud cake 110
 pistachio, white chocolate and
  honey french macaroons 180
 white chocolate and berry
  cheesecake slice 224

Y
yogurt 251